GAFFE/STUTTER

Gaffe/Stutter

Whitney Anne Trettien

dead letter office

BABEL Working Group

punctum books * brooklyn, ny

GAFFE/STUTTER
© Whitney Anne Trettien, 2013

http://creativecommons.org/licenses/by-nc-nd/3.0/

This work is Open Access, which means that you are free to copy, distribute, display, and perform the work as long as you clearly attribute the work to the authors, that you do not use this work for commercial gain in any form whatsoever, and that you in no way alter, transform, or build upon the work outside of its normal use in academic scholarship without express permission of the author and the publisher of this volume. For any reuse or distribution, you must make clear to other the license terms of this work.

First published in 2013 by
dead letter office, BABEL Working Group
an imprint of punctum books
Brooklyn, New York
http://punctumbooks.com

The BABEL Working Group is a collective and desiring-assemblage of scholar-gypsies with no leaders or followers, no top and no bottom, and only a middle. BABEL roams and stalks the ruins of the post-historical university as a multiplicity, a pack, looking for other roaming packs and multiplicities with which to cohabit and build temporary shelters for intellectual vagabonds. We also take in strays.

ISBN-13: 978-0615877488
ISBN-10: 0615877486

gaffestutter.com: website design by Whiney Anne Trettien

Visit **GAFFESTUTTER.COM**

Past (*continued*)
    77; unlimited, 61-62; untimely in relation to, 265
Past perfect, of the alcoholic, 158-59, 160
Péguy, Charles, 53, 340n5
Penis, 200-1, 202, 204, 205, 206, 227, 237; absence of, 228, 243; bad/good, 200; internal, 204, 205
Perception, 318; noema in, 20-21; presence of Others and, 305-6, 307, 308-9; consciousness system, 203; perceptual hold, 308-9, 318; Other as structure of, 307-10
Perrier, Edmund, 355n3

Gaffe

←

Men may dream in demonstrations, and cut out an illusory world in the shape of axioms, definitions, and propositions, with a final exclusion of fact signed Q. E. D. No formulas for thinking will save us mortals from mistake in our imperfect apprehension of the matter to be thought about. And since the unemotional intellect may carry us into a mathematical dream-land where nothing is but what is not, perhaps an emotional intellect may have absorbed into its passionate vision of possibilities some truth of what will be — the more comprehensive massive life feeding theory with new material, as the sensibility of the artist seizes combinations which science explains and justifies.

At any rate, presumptions to the contrary are not to be trusted.

– George Eliot, *Daniel Deronda*

GAFFE ←

Twelve or so people came to the first meeting of the Logic of Sense reading group, paper copies of the "First Series of Paradoxes of Pure Becoming" crackling in their hands.

My memory of the meeting inheres in its configuration: bare knees under a plastic tabletop, a backpack slumped below; my friend's black fountain pen, poised over the blazing white page.

As we worked our way through the chapter, his hand kept urging his pen toward the paper, eager to materialize some evidence that he understood the text, that it **MADE SENSE;** but something blocked words from forming.

He – we, all of us – littered our margins with ink blots, lin*e*s, the <u>occasional</u> <u>asterisk</u> noting a flash of insight since lost; claw marks from a pack hungry for meaning.

Desire for
knowledge
had held together
a series of objects
that the charge of
awkwardness
eventually
dispelled;
and by
the
group's
third
meeting,
attendance had plunged to four people,
where it more or
less stayed for the
next twenty weeks.

We were an odd bunch, comprised of the professor who had initiated the group, with whom I was taking a pleasurably labyrinthine, if slightly incomprehensible class on ecology, realism and gift-giving; a third-year in the English PhD program with an affinity for Guattari, and a warmness toward Deleuze by association; a recent graduate of the Literature program and the sharpest reader of Continental philosophy I'd ever met; and me. Looking back, it seems odd that I stuck with it. Yet like my friend's hand, urging his pen to paper, something pushed me to seek out these regular encounters with nonsense.

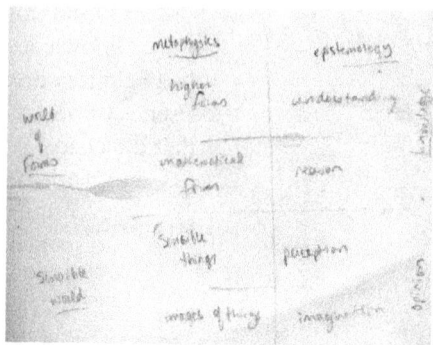

Figure 1. Today's task is to make the empty square circulate and to make pre-individual and nonpersonal singularities speak – in short, to produce sense

Our meetings came to form the horizon of my week – an experience I was always simultaneously both approaching and retreating from.

From my vantage point, I could *see* a boundary point in the distance, could even assign it a signifier like 'horizon'; but this frontier was an impossible meeting of sky and earth, illusively produced by the space I inhabited and my own stance within it. Because this space was so singular, speaking – a fundamentally *communal* activity – felt impossible, *having no subject which expresses or manifests itself in it, no object to denote, no classes and no properties to signify according to a fixed order.* So I observed instead. I especially enjoyed watching the Recent Graduate talk – how he framed phrases in the air, then looped them together into unicursal mazes of thought, bafflingly complex in their form yet wholly comprehensible. The Professor didn't talk like the Recent Graduate but instead tried to pin down *terms*: what *bodies* are, what *manifestation* is, bulleted lists of expressions (see Figure 1). His was a different, more reasoned relationship to the material, one that I respect in its own right; but, still: listening to the Professor talk made feel as if I could never make sense of Deleuze's logic, and would never want to anyway (of what relevance?). Listening to the Recent Graduate, though, was more like watching crystals *become and grow out of the edges.*

One could say that the old depth

I checked out books on Logic of Sense, books like James Williams's Gilles Deleuze's Logic of Sense: A Critical Introduction and Guide. These are profoundly learned yet fundamentally *absurd* projects, pulled in one direction by their medium and by their message in another. As these guidebooks will readily affirm, Deleuze's book does not comment on Alice in Wonderland but *rewrites* it. That is, there's no place for annotation in its world, no marginal space waiting to be filled with pithy summation; there is only the infinite regress of repetition with a difference — only the same chapter, the same *point* reproduced along a 34-item series. Only trained academics could enter this hall of mirrors and, instead of warping the presence of their own bodies — larger, smaller, one's image constantly eluding the present — drop a paper trail, so as not to lose their way home.

I'm being too harsh. Observing how another person wades through a text as dense as Logic of Sense can be illuminating — but only obliquely, with the scattered radiance of a raking light on the page's surface. And I'm more of the flashlight-in-the-hall-of-mirrors type. Insight comes from the disorienting blindness of confusion, and the struggle to find a new sense with which to *make* sense. If I couldn't speak, I had to find another way.

So I began to sketch. I drew diagrams, concepts, the vectors between them; machines for the production of sense and for the survey of the surface. Graph paper enabled a relationship with the text that the book's margins had foreclosed, carving out a space for a material engagement not possible in the mist of conversation. *If you say something, it passes through your lips*, Deleuze quotes of Chryssipus; *so, if you say 'chariot,' a chariot passes through your lips*. To sketch was to force a chariot through my lips, replacing the depth of language with the surface of the grid.

And then —

GAFFE

I heard an ad on the radio this week.

It was for _____, 'the windshield experts.' They talked about how it's dangerous to drive around with a crack in your window — I mean a crack from a rock or something; because it might have caused imperceptible damage, hairline cracks in the glass that spread out from the edge. One day, you'll be driving along, then boom, your windshield caves in. All because you followed a garbage truck too closely six months ago.

It is imperceptible, incorporeal, and ideational.

We were discussing cracks in the "Twenty-Second Series: Porcelain and Volcano" – surface cracks; imperceptible fissures skimming the tops of Events. The Professor was analogizing Deleuze's image to a cracked egg, to cement, images layered over images, while the Recent Graduate poked his finger forcefully into the book's gutter.

Everything noisy happens at the edge of the crack, Deleuze writes, *and would be nothing without it*. If there was noise, it was white noise, rushing in my ears; if there was a crack, it was the kind of crack only _____ could fix: imperceptible and yet persistent; dangerous. *The real difference is not between the inside and the outside*, I read, *for the crack is neither internal nor external, but rather at the frontier.*

GAFFE

Our reading group petered out shortly after that meeting. Summer happened; travel happened, dissertations happened, books happened, job-hunting and jobs happened. My primary field of study is book history, and book historians don't read Deleuze much. Life flowed forward.

In a last-ditch effort to salvage something tangible from the experience – something other than inkblots and graph paper and incomprehensible annotations – I began planning a web-based diagrammatic (r)e(n)dition of <u>Logic of Sense</u>. Before I had begun to code, the project had already become elaborately impossible. At its center (I imagined) would be high-resolution scans of the diagrams I had been producing; these, then, would be zoomable and annotatable in both text and image, such that any online visitor could respond to my diagram with one of their own. In other words it was to be an anti-book: a visual reading schematic that eschewed the line of text in favor of regimented grids, the ink-soaked grain of the remediated pen over the laser-burned face of print; playful reaction rather than academic protraction. *This is not an analogy, or a product of the imagination*, Gilles Deleuze and Felix Guattari would write in <u>A Thousand Plateaus</u>, *but a composition of speeds and affects on the plane of consistency: a plan(e), a program, or rather a diagram, a problem, a question-machine.*

Yet question-machines are easier to produce in printed books – of the type that Deleuze and Guattari produced – than in code. Though our daily experience of web browsing is increasingly dynamic, the compilation of markup and scripts that engineer this experience is text-based and rigidly hierarchical. The <HEAD> of each webpage defines its organs – what to call them, how they'll look, how they'll move together – and the <BODY>

(proceeding downward, in anatomical fashion) contains the organs being defined in their proper order. While the ordering of each part can be changed by redefining its "z-index" in the `<HEAD>`, the `<BODY>` defaults to a linear left-to-right, top-to-bottom sequence, such that the organ that appears first in the body's markup will appear in the top left corner of the page – just as in a printed book.

In other words, in my attempt to create a multi-planar, diagrammatic anti-book, I had actually turned to one of the most strictly sequential media structures ever devised. Like the critical guides I had found so frustratingly paradoxical, my website was to be torn apart limb from limb the moment it came into existence.

Given this, it's no surprise to me that this project failed to reach completion. I had started prototyping with pre-fabricated platforms like Wordpress or Omeka but quickly realized that these systems could only define my drawings according to the type of media object they were, rather than the use I imagined for them. jQuery plug-ins, which I turned to next, were similarly limiting. While writing code that zooms and pans across large images is easy enough, getting these snippets of code to play nice with some form of annotation system that stores user input was beyond my level of skill at the time. Thus although it was once an active space for testing new assemblages of code, the 'logicofsense' directory on my server is now a graveyard of inert demos: an image of Trafalgar Square at dusk, annotated with the words "Flag," "Small people on the steps," "A Statue," and "National Gallery Dome"; an empty HTML file titled 'delete.html'.

Over the course of a few months, I spent less and less time trying to configure the elements into a functional project. And, since working on the website had interrupted my sketch-reading, I stopped drawing too, which all but ended my dives into the dark and immaterial depths of each paradox. I knew the project was finally dead when I received an email from a reading group in Baltimore that wanted me to cede ownership of the abandoned Wordpress account "LogicOfSense" so that they could start a page for their own discussions. After some administrative wrangling, I managed to transfer ownership to them. Though I presume they flourished there for a time, the site is now also, and again, defunct. It seems the Baltimore reading group didn't just abandon the project, as I had, but destroyed all evidence that it ever existed, leaving only a standard Wordpress notice: "The authors have deleted this site."

The state in which I left my own page is the state in which it remains today: that is, a single image, my first drawing, can be zoomed and panned using two magnifying glass icons in the bottom right corner of the screen, and two red rectangles adorn the top corners of the page but do nothing, link nowhere. The visitor who may happen to wander into this dead-end corner of the web would find herself sstuck on Deleuze's definition of a paradox as *initially that which destroys good sense as the only direction* of becoming, but *also that which destroys common sense as the assignation of fixed identities*. Alice is larger now; she was smaller before.

*Alice does **not grow** without shrinking, and vice versa.*

This is the simultaneity of a becoming,
    we read,
           whose characteristic is to elude

the present.
   One could object that all of this means nothing. It is a bad play on words to suppose that nonsense expresses its own sense, since, by definition, *it has none.*

never state the sense of what I am saying. But on the other hand, I can always take the sense of what I say as the object of another proposition whose sense, in turn, I cannot state. I thus enter into the infinite regress of that which is presupposed.

— Gilles Deleuze, "Fifth Series of Sense," *Logic of Sense*

Stutter

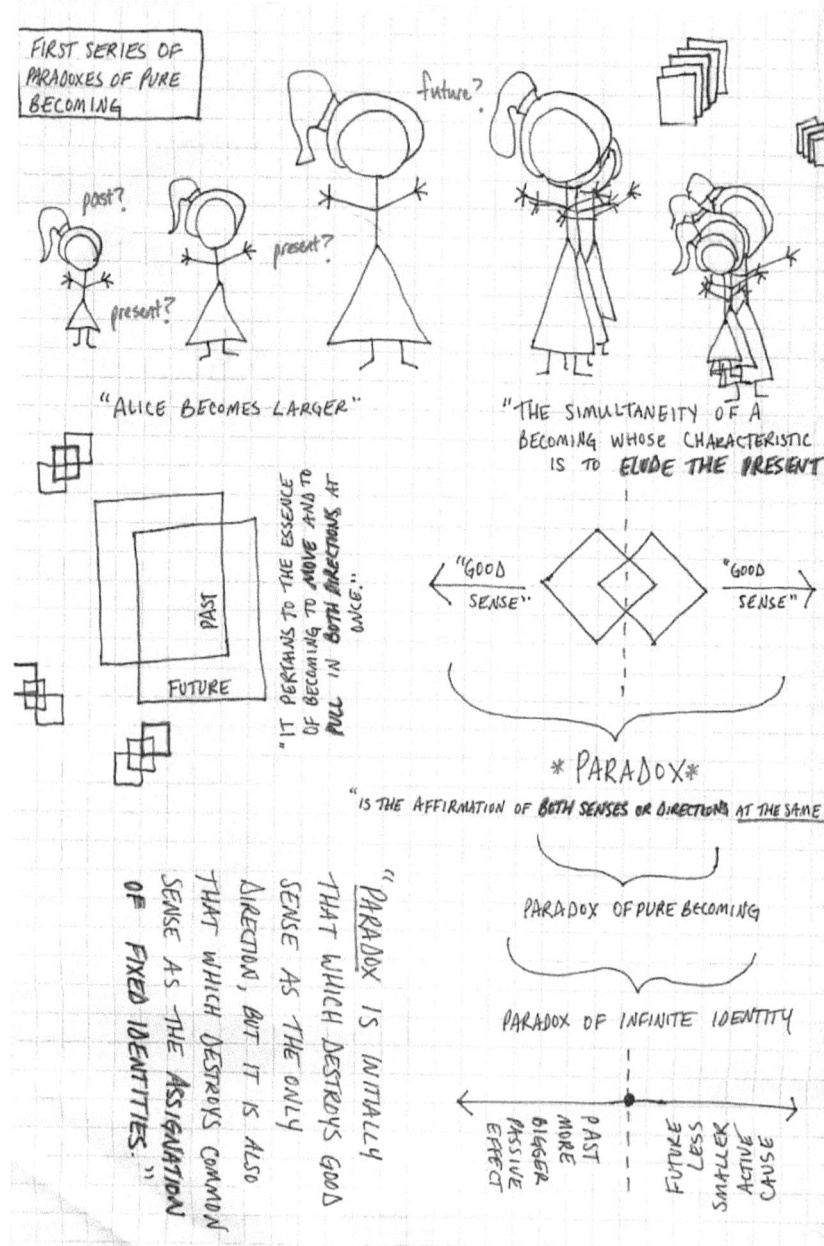

demo-static.html

```html
<html>
    <head>
        <title>Image Annotations</title>
        <style type="text/css" media="all">@import
"css/annotation.css";</style>
        <script type="text/javascript"
src="js/jquery-1.3.2.js"></script>
        <script type="text/javascript"
src="js/jquery-ui-1.7.1.js"></script>
        <script type="text/javascript"
src="js/jquery.annotate.js"></script>

        <script language="javascript">
            $(window).load(function() {
                $("#toAnnotate").annotateImage({
                    editable: true,
                    useAjax: false,
                    notes: [ { "top": 286,
                                "left": 161,
                                "width": 52,
                                "height": 37,
                                "text": "Small
people on the steps",
                                "id": "e69213d0-
2eef-40fa-a04b-0ed998f9f1f5",
                                "editable": false
},
                             { "top": 134,
                                "left": 179,
                                "width": 68,
                                "height": 74,
                                "text": "National
Gallery Dome",
                                "id": "e7f44ac5-
bcf2-412d-b440-6dbb8b19ffbe",
                                "editable": true
} ]
                });
            });
        </script>
    </head>
    <body>
        <div>
            <img id="toAnnotate"
src="images/trafalgar-square-annotated.jpg"
alt="Trafalgar Square" width="600" height="398" />
        </div>
    </body>
</html>
```

delete.html

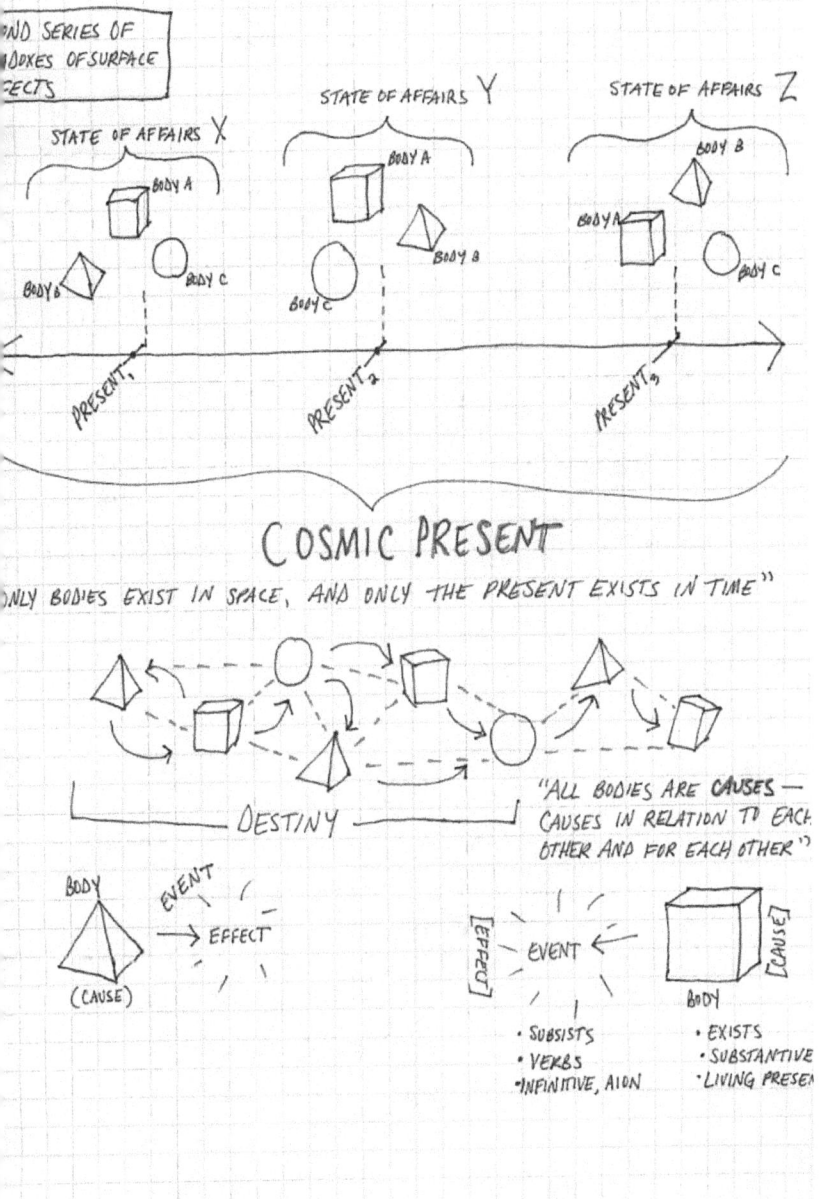

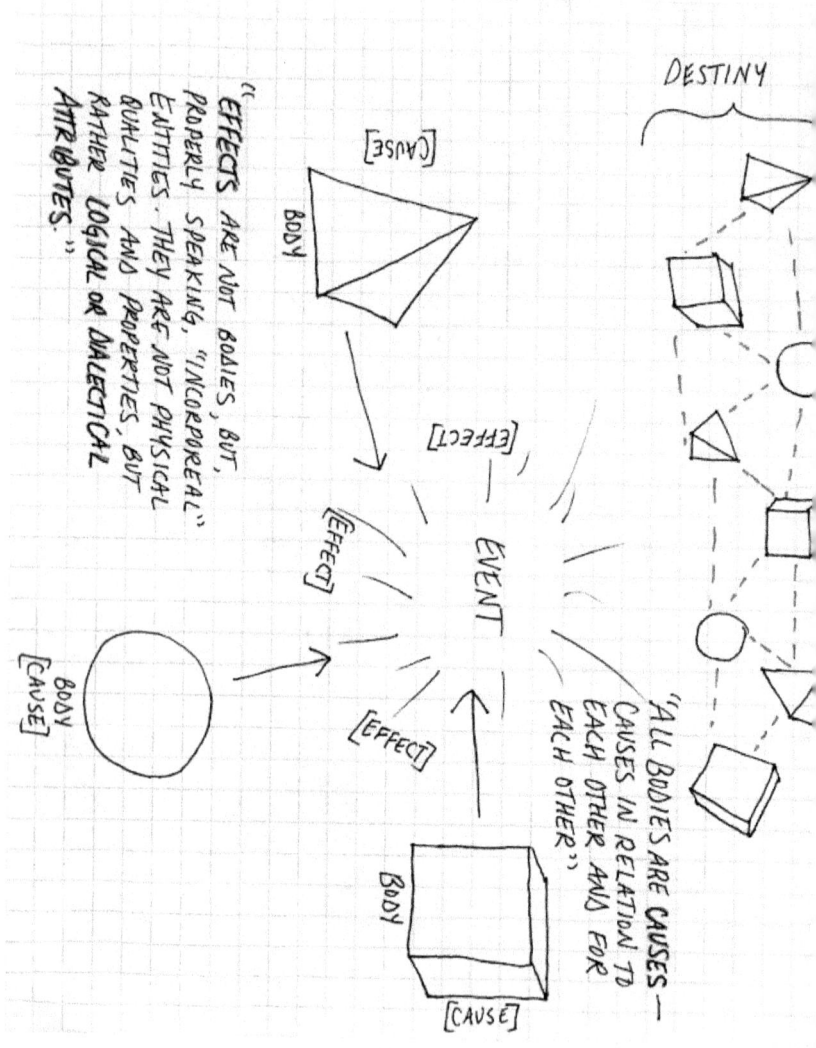

get.html

```
[
  { "top": 286, "left": 161, "width": 52,
  "height": 37, "text": "Small people on the
  steps", "id": "e69213d0-2eef-40fa-a04b-
  0ed998f9f1f5", "editable": false },
  { "top": 134, "left": 179, "width": 68,
  "height": 74, "text": "National Gallery
  Dome", "id": "e7f44ac5-bcf2-412d-b440-
  6dbb8b19ffbe", "editable": true },
  { "top": 164, "left": 41, "width": 35,
  "height": 60, "text": "Flag", "id":
  "8823747f-c306-4c1c-ac00-09580bd1012f",
  "editable": false },
  { "top": 167, "left": 538, "width": 60,
  "height": 90, "text": "A statue ", "id":
  "e68126e9-7785-46a2-9680-852c8d618c60",
  "editable": true }
]
```

magnify1.gif

magnify2.gif

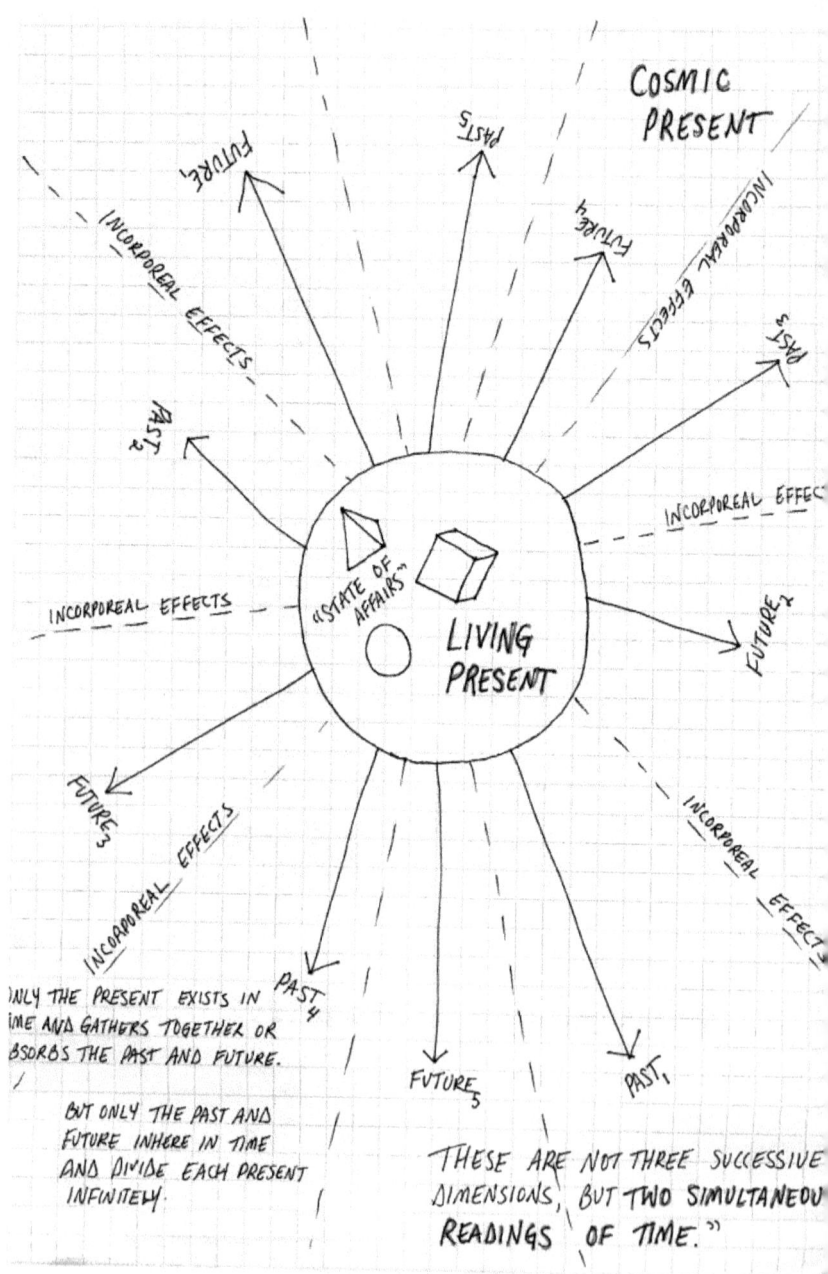

shiftzoom.js

```
/**
 * shiftzoom.js 3.2 (16-Sep-2009) (c) by Christian Effenberger
 * All Rights Reserved. Source: shiftzoom.netzgesta.de
 * Distributed under Netzgestade Software License Agreement.
 * This license permits free of charge use on non-commercial
 * and private web sites only under special conditions.
 * Read more at... http://www.netzgesta.de/cvi/LICENSE.txt
 *
 * syntax:
    shiftzoom.defaultFading = true;      //BOOLEAN startup fading
    shiftzoom.defaultButtons = true;     //BOOLEAN left top info & zoom buttons
    shiftzoom.defaultNozoom = false;     //BOOLEAN disable zooming feature
    shiftzoom.defaultBicubic = false;    //BOOLEAN enable MS bicubic image interpolation mode for IE7+
    shiftzoom.defaultZoom = 0;           //INT/FLOAT 0-100 (%) zooming percentage
    shiftzoom.defaultXpos = 50;          //INT/FLOAT 0-100 (%) horizontal position
    shiftzoom.defaultYpos = 50;          //INT/FLOAT 0-100 (%) vertical position
    shiftzoom.defaultOpacity = 90;       //INT 0-100 (%) zoom button opacity
    shiftzoom.defaultMillisec = 40;      //INT 5-100 zoom interval delay
    shiftzoom.defaultIntitle = '';       //STR 'click or press shift key to zoom in'
    shiftzoom.defaultOuttitle = '';      //STR 'click or press alt key to zoom out'
    shiftzoom.defaultInfoblock = '';     //STR
'<dl><div align="right">Mouseover <big>Keyboard Support<\/big><\/div><dt>Zoom in:<\/dt><dd>[+] / [PgDn] / [End] <em>(is faster)<\/em> /<br \/> [shift] + <u>left</u> mouse button /<br \/><u>middle</u> / <u>wheel</u> mouse button /<br \/>mouse wheel <u>down</u><small><br \/><br \/><\/small><\/dd><dt>Zoom out:<\/dt><dd>[-] / [PgUp] / [Home] <em>(is faster)<\/em> /<br \/> [alt] + <u>left</u> mouse button /<br \/><u>right</u> mouse button /<br \/>mouse wheel <u>up</u><small><br
```

```
\/><br \/><\/small><\/dd><dt>Pan / Shift /
Move:<\/dt><dd>[left] / [right] / [down] / [up]
arrow buttons<br \/>+ [shift] <em>(is faster)<\/em>
and + [alt] <em>(is slower)<\/em><\/dd><\/dl>'
     shiftzoom.defaultCurpath = '';       //STR
cursor path (*.cur) IE only
     shiftzoom.defaultLowres = '';        //STR
lowres image (dimension should equal elements width
and height)
     shiftzoom.defaultIcons = null;       //OBJ icon
array (see shiftzoom.construct)
     shiftzoom.defaultShowcoords = false;//BOOLEAN
show coordinates
     shiftzoom.defaultPixelcoords = true;//BOOLEAN
Pixel instead of Latitude/Longitude coordinates
     shiftzoom.defaultPercentcoords=false;//BOOLEAN
Percentage instead of Lat/Lon/Pixel coordinates
     shiftzoom.defaultOverview = true;    //BOOLEAN
show overview
     shiftzoom.defaultOvsfact = 25;       //INT 10-50
(%) overview size percentage
     shiftzoom.defaultOvaopac = 75;       //INT 0-100
(%) overview area opacity
     shiftzoom.defaultOvacolor = 'red';   //STR
overview area css color
     shiftzoom.defaultOvbcolor = 'white';//STR
overview border css color
     shiftzoom.defaultOvborder = '';      //INT 0-20
(px) or "" overview border width
     shiftzoom.add( image, options );
     shiftzoom.add( image, { fading: value, buttons:
value, nozoom: value, zoom: value, xpos: value,
ypos: value, overview: value, curpath: value,
intitle: value, outtitle: value, millisec: value,
ovaopac: value, opacity: value, ovborder: value,
ovacolor: value, ovbcolor: value, ovsfact: value }
);
     shiftzoom.remove( image, value );    //BOOLEAN
reset to max image width/height
     shiftzoom.source( image, URI, value );
//BOOLEAN with fading
     shiftzoom.lowsource( image, URI );
     shiftzoom.set( image,
['buttons'|'overview'|'showcoords'|'pixelcoords'|'pe
rcentcoords'|'zoomin'|'zoomout'|'nozoom'],
[true|false] );
INT=shiftzoom.get( image,
['maxzoomx'|'maxzoomy'|'maxwidth'|'maxheight'] );
BOL=shiftzoom.get( image, 'playing' );
OBJ=shiftzoom.get( image, 'currentxyz' );//returns
current x=Xpos, y=Ypos and z=Zoom as INT/FLOAT 0-100
```

━━━━━━━━━━━━━━━━━━▶ **STUTTER**

```
(%)
FLT=shiftzoom.version;
STR=shiftzoom.released;
    shiftzoom.zooming( image, value );    //INT 0 -
100 (%) zoom factor (e.g. 33.33)
    shiftzoom.moveto( image, x, y );      //INT x|y
from within natural image dimension (e.g. 400,297)
or
                                          //STR
Lon|Lat (e.g. '52.04','-23.4405') or
                                          //STR
%|% (e.g. '50%','50%')
    shiftzoom.kenburns( image, [x, y, z, e, s, d,
callback, arg] ); //INT x|y|z 0 - 100 (%) move/zoom
factor
                                          //FLT
0-2|3 e == progression [< 1 == ease-out | 1 ==
linear | > 1 == ease-in | 3 == ease-in-out]
(default: 1) optional (set to false for default
value if you want to use callback)
                                          //INT
10-100 s equals animation steps (default: auto
equals max distance/interval delay) optional (set to
false for default value if you want to use callback)
                                          //INT
10-100 d equals interval delay (default: 30)
optional (set to false for default value if you want
to use callback)
                                          //STR
callback function name (executes on end playing)
                                          //STR
arg callback function argument
    shiftzoom.play( image, delay, loop, array,
callback ); //INT delay between anims (millisec)
        //BOOLEAN endless loop or once
                                          //OBJ
two dimensional Array [[x,y,z,e,s,d],
[x,y,z,e,s,d]...] (syntax like kenburns)
                                          //STR
callback function name (executes on stop playing)
    shiftzoom.stop( image );              //stop auto
playing
    shiftzoom.construct( image, object ); //create
icon object(s)
    object = [{x:INT, y:INT, w:INT, h:INT, pos:INT,
noscale:BOL, id:'STR', href:'STR', target:'STR',
title:'STR', src:'STR', src2:'STR'}, {...}]
        pos equals 1=left-top, 2=center-top,
3=right-top, 4=center-left, 0/5=center, 6=center-
right, 7=left-bottom, 8=center-bottom, 9=right-
bottom
```

```
            if noscale is true (fixed icon
    dimensions), pos equals always left-top
        shiftzoom.destruct( image, id|true ); //delete
    named or all icon(s)
     *
    **/
    var cvi_sztimer, cvi_szactive, cvi_szimage=null,
    shiftzoom = { _shiftzoom : null, version : 3.2,
    released : '2009-09-16 16:11:00',
        defaultFading : true, defaultButtons : true,
    defaultOverview : true, defaultNozoom : false,
    defaultIcons : null, defaultBicubic : false,
        defaultShowcoords : false, defaultPixelcoords :
    true, defaultPercentcoords : false, defaultLowres :
    '', defaultMillisec : 40,
        defaultOpacity : 90, defaultOvsfact : 25,
    defaultOvaopac : 75, defaultOvacolor : 'red',
    defaultOvbcolor : 'white',
        defaultIntitle : 'click or press shift key to
    zoom in', defaultOuttitle : 'click or press alt key
    to zoom out',
        defaultInfoblock : '<dl><div
    align="right">Mouseover <big>Keyboard
    Support<\/big><\/div><dt>Zoom in:<\/dt><dd>[+] /
    [PgDn] / [End] <em>(is faster)<\/em> /<br \/>
    [shift] + <u>left</u> mouse button /<br
    \/><u>middle</u> / <u>wheel</u> mouse button /<br
    \/>mouse wheel <u>down</u><small><br \/><br
    \/><\/small><\/dd><dt>Zoom out:<\/dt><dd>[-] /
    [PgUp] / [Home] <em>(is faster)<\/em> /<br \/> [alt]
    + <u>left</u> mouse button /<br \/><u>right</u>
    mouse button /<br \/>mouse wheel <u>up</u><small><br
    \/><br \/><\/small><\/dd><dt>Pan / Shift /
    Move:<\/dt><dd>[left] / [right] / [down] / [up]
    arrow buttons<br \/>+ [shift] <em>(is faster)</em>
    and + [alt] <em>(is slower)<\/em><\/dd><\/dl>',
        defaultOvborder : '', defaultCurpath : '',
    defaultZoom : 0, defaultXpos : 50, defaultYpos : 50,
        gif :
    "data:image/gif;base64,R0lGOD1hAQABAJH/AP///wAAAP///
    wAAACH/C0FETOJFOklSMS4wAt7tACH5BAEAAAIALAAAAAABAAEAA
    AICVAEAOw==",
        add : function(ele,opts) {
            function roundTo(val,dig) {var num=val;
    if(val>8191&&val<10485) {val=val-5000;
    num=Math.round(val*Math.pow(10,dig))/Math.pow(10,dig
    ); num=num+5000;}else
    {num=Math.round(val*Math.pow(10,dig))/Math.pow(10,di
    g);} return num;}
            function uniqueID() {var val=Date.parse(new
    Date())+Math.floor(Math.random()*100000000000);
```

```
return val.toString(16);}
        function boxShadow() {var
bs=false,mbs=false,kbs=false,wbs=false; try
{bs=(document.body.style.boxShadow!==undefined);}cat
ch(e) {} try
{mbs=(document.body.style.MozBoxShadow!==undefined);
}catch(e) {} try
{kbs=(document.body.style.KhtmlBoxShadow!==undefined
);}catch(e) {} try
{wbs=(document.body.style.WebkitBoxShadow!==undefine
d);}catch(e) {} return
(bs||mbs||kbs||wbs?true:false);}
        if(!ele.active)
{ele.style.visibility="hidden";
            var defopts={"curpath" :
shiftzoom.defaultCurpath, "opacity" :
shiftzoom.defaultOpacity, "millisec" :
shiftzoom.defaultMillisec, "intitle" :
shiftzoom.defaultIntitle, "outtitle" :
shiftzoom.defaultOuttitle, "infoblock" :
shiftzoom.defaultInfoblock, "ovsfact" :
shiftzoom.defaultOvsfact, "ovaopac" :
shiftzoom.defaultOvaopac, "ovacolor" :
shiftzoom.defaultOvacolor, "ovbcolor" :
shiftzoom.defaultOvbcolor, "zoom" :
shiftzoom.defaultZoom, "xpos" :
shiftzoom.defaultXpos, "ypos" :
shiftzoom.defaultYpos, "lowres" :
shiftzoom.defaultLowres, "icons" :
shiftzoom.defaultIcons, "bicubic" :
shiftzoom.defaultBicubic };
            if(opts) {for(var i in
defopts){if(!opts[i]){opts[i]=defopts[i];}}}else{opt
s=defopts;}
    if(document.images&&document.createElement&&doc
ument.getElementById&&document.getElementsByTagName)
{
                var
st,over,view,div=ele.parentNode,img=shiftzoom.E('div
'),xref=shiftzoom.E('img'),outer=shiftzoom.E('div');
img.xid=(ele.id!=""?ele.id:ele.id=uniqueID());
                div.appendChild(outer);
outer.id=img.xid+'_wrap'; outer.appendChild(xref);
outer.appendChild(img); img.wrapid=outer.id;
img.opts=defopts; img.highres=ele.src;
                if(ele.naturalWidth &&
ele.naturalHeight)
{img.xfactor=roundTo(ele.naturalWidth/ele.width,4);
img.yfactor=roundTo(ele.naturalHeight/ele.height,4);
img.maxwidth=ele.naturalWidth;
img.maxheight=ele.naturalHeight;}
```

```
            else {var tmp=new Image;
tmp.src=ele.src;
img.xfactor=roundTo(tmp.width/ele.width,4);
img.yfactor=roundTo(tmp.height/ele.height,4);
img.maxwidth=tmp.width; img.maxheight=tmp.height;
tmp=null; delete tmp;}
     if(ele.width>=100&&ele.width<img.maxwidth&&ele.
height>=100&&ele.height<img.maxheight){
                    img.fading=(typeof
opts['fading']==='boolean'?opts['fading']:shiftzoom.
defaultFading);
                    img.buttons=(typeof
opts['buttons']==='boolean'?opts['buttons']:shiftzoo
m.defaultButtons);
                    img.nozoom=(typeof
opts['nozoom']==='boolean'?opts['nozoom']:shiftzoom.
defaultNozoom);
                    img.bicubic=(typeof
opts['bicubic']==='boolean'?opts['bicubic']:shiftzoo
m.defaultBicubic);
                    img.overview=(typeof
opts['overview']==='boolean'?opts['overview']:shiftz
oom.defaultOverview);
                    img.showcoords=(typeof
opts['showcoords']==='boolean'?opts['showcoords']:sh
iftzoom.defaultShowcoords);
                    img.pixelcoords=(typeof
opts['pixelcoords']==='boolean'?opts['pixelcoords']:
shiftzoom.defaultPixelcoords);
                    img.percentcoords=(typeof
opts['percentcoords']==='boolean'?opts['percentcoord
s']:shiftzoom.defaultPercentcoords);
                    img.lowres=(typeof
opts['lowres']==='string'?opts['lowres']:img.opts['l
owres']);
                    img.icons=(typeof
opts['icons']==='object'?opts['icons']:img.opts['ico
ns']); img.bicubic=(img.bicubic?"bicubic":"nearest-
neighbor");
                    img.curpath=(typeof
opts['curpath']==='string'?opts['curpath']:img.opts[
'curpath']);
                    img.intitle=(typeof
opts['intitle']==='string'?opts['intitle']:img.opts[
'intitle']);
                    img.outtitle=(typeof
opts['outtitle']==='string'?opts['outtitle']:img.opt
s['outtitle']);
                    img.infoblock=(typeof
opts['infoblock']==='string'?opts['infoblock']:img.o
pts['infoblock']); img.defblock=img.infoblock;
```

```
                        img.ovacolor=(typeof
opts['ovacolor']==='string'?opts['ovacolor']:img.opt
s['ovacolor']);
                        img.ovbcolor=(typeof
opts['ovbcolor']==='string'?opts['ovbcolor']:img.opt
s['ovbcolor']);
                        img.ovsfact=(typeof
opts['ovsfact']==='number'?parseInt(Math.min(Math.ma
x(10,opts['ovsfact']),50)):img.opts['ovsfact'])/100;
                        img.millisec=(typeof
opts['millisec']==='number'?parseInt(Math.min(Math.m
ax(5,opts['millisec']),100)):img.opts['millisec']);
                        img.ovaopac=(typeof
opts['ovaopac']==='number'?parseInt(Math.min(Math.ma
x(0,opts['ovaopac']),100)):img.opts['ovaopac']);
                        img.opacity=(typeof
opts['opacity']==='number'?parseInt(Math.min(Math.ma
x(0,opts['opacity']),100)):img.opts['opacity']);
                        img.ovborder=(typeof
opts['ovborder']==='number'?parseInt(Math.min(Math.m
ax(0,opts['ovborder']),20)):Math.min(Math.round(ele.
width/100),Math.round(ele.height/100)));
                        img.zoom=(typeof
opts['zoom']==='number'?parseFloat(Math.min(Math.max
(0,opts['zoom']),100)):img.opts['zoom']);
                        img.xpos=(typeof
opts['xpos']==='number'?parseFloat(Math.min(Math.max
(0,opts['xpos']),100)):img.opts['xpos']);
                        img.ypos=(typeof
opts['ypos']==='number'?parseFloat(Math.min(Math.max
(0,opts['ypos']),100)):img.opts['ypos']);
                        img.opts=null; defopts=null;
img.bc="1px white solid"; img.dc="1px gray solid";
img.automode=false; img.autoloop=false;
img.autowait=0; img.zoomin=false; img.zoomout=false;
                        st=ele.parentNode.style;
st.position=(st.position=='static'||st.position==''?
'relative':st.position); st.height=ele.height+'px';
st.width=ele.width+'px';
                        st.padding='0px';
st.overflow='hidden'; st.MozUserSelect="none";
st.KhtmlUserSelect="none";
ele.parentNode.unselectable="on"; st.border="none";
                        outer.unselectable="on";
outer.left=0; outer.top=0; outer.width=ele.width;
outer.height=ele.height; st=outer.style;
st.MozUserSelect="none"; st.KhtmlUserSelect="none";
                        st.visibility="hidden";
st.display="block"; st.position="absolute";
st.left='0px'; st.top='0px';
st.width=ele.width+'px'; st.height=ele.height+'px';
```

```
                        xref.id=img.xid+'_img';
xref.src=ele.src; st=xref.style;
st.msInterpolationMode=img.bicubic;
st.position="absolute"; st.left='0px'; st.top='0px';
                        st.width='100%';
st.height='100%'; img.xrefid=xref.id;
img.unselectable="on"; st=img.style;
st.MozUserSelect="none"; st.KhtmlUserSelect="none";
                        st.display="block";
st.position="relative";
if(document.all&&!window.opera){st.background="url('"
+img.curpath+"nop.gif') transparent";}
                        st.left='0px'; st.top='0px';
st.width='100%'; st.height='100%';
st.cursor="crosshair"; img.pointer=st.cursor;
img.minwidth=outer.width;
                        img.minheight=outer.height;
img.maxleft=img.maxwidth-img.minwidth;
img.maxtop=img.maxheight-img.minheight; ele.id="";
outer.parentNode.removeChild(ele); img.id=img.xid;
                        if(img.fading)
{if(img.trident)
{outer.style.filter="alpha(opacity=0)";}else{outer.s
tyle.opacity=0;}} outer.style.visibility='visible';
    img.trident=document.all&&!window.opera?1:0;
img.notrans=img.trident&&!window.XMLHttpRequest?1:0;
    img.webkit=window.atob!=undefined&&!window.upda
teCommands?1:0;
img.divbug=!img.webkit&&navigator.userAgent.indexOf(
'WebKit')>-1?1:0;
    img.gecko=navigator.userAgent.indexOf('Gecko')>
-1&&window.updateCommands?1:0;
img.presto=window.opera?1:0;
img.bshadow=boxShadow();
    img.bmode=(img.trident&&(document.compatMode=='
BackCompat'||document.compatMode=='QuirksMode')?true
:false); img.active=true;
                        over=shiftzoom.E('img');
over.src=img.trident?null:null;
over.style.display='none'; over.id=img.id+'_isrc';
div.appendChild(over); img.isrcid=over.id;
                        over=shiftzoom.E('div');
over.id=img.id+'_xyco'; st=over.style;
if(img.trident) {st.backgroundColor='black';}
st.height='auto'; st.width='auto';
                        st.display='block';
st.position='absolute'; st.left='0px';
st.bottom='0px'; st.MozUserSelect="none";
st.KhtmlUserSelect="none"; over.unselectable="on";
    if(img.fading&&img.showcoords||!img.showcoords)
{st.visibility='hidden';} st.cursor='help';
```

STUTTER

```
div.appendChild(over); img.xycoid=over.id;
                    if(!img.trident) {var
view=shiftzoom.E('div'); st=view.style;
st.height='100%'; st.width='100%'; st.left='0px';
st.bottom='0px'; st.position='absolute';
st.backgroundColor='black'; st.opacity=0.5;
over.appendChild(view);}
                    view=shiftzoom.E('div');
view.id=img.id+'_cpos'; view.innerHTML="x:0 y:0";
view.unselectable="on"; st=view.style;
st.textAlign='left'; st.verticalAlign='middle';
st.left='0px'; st.bottom='0px';
                    st.position='relative';
st.display='block'; st.color='white';
st.fontSize='10px'; st.fontFamily='Arial, Helvetica,
sans-serif'; st.fontStyle='normal';
                    st.fontWeight='bold';
st.whiteSpace='nowrap'; st.padding='2px 4px';
st.textShadow='0px 0px 4px black';
over.appendChild(view); img.cposid=view.id;
                    over=shiftzoom.E('div');
st=over.style;
if(img.fading&&img.buttons||!img.buttons)
{st.visibility='hidden';} over.id=img.id+'_ctrl';
st.height='16px';
                    st.width='42px';
st.display="block"; st.position='absolute';
st.lineHeight='1px'; st.fontSize='1px';
st.backgroundColor="#cccccc";
                    if(img.trident)
{st.filter="alpha(opacity="+img.opacity+")";}else{st
.opacity=img.opacity/100;} st.cursor='pointer';
st.left='0px'; st.top='0px'; st.boxShadow="0px 0px
8px black";
                    st.MozBoxShadow="0px 0px 8px
black"; st.KhtmlBoxShadow="0px 0px 8px black";
st.WebkitBoxShadow="0px 0px 8px black";
div.appendChild(over); img.ctrlid=over.id;
                    view=shiftzoom.E('div');
st=view.style; st.height='2px'; st.width='2px';
st.position='absolute'; st.lineHeight='1px';
st.fontSize='1px'; st.left='4px'; st.top='3px';
st.backgroundColor="black"; over.appendChild(view);
                    view=shiftzoom.E('div');
st=view.style; st.height='6px'; st.width='2px';
st.position='absolute'; st.lineHeight='1px';
st.fontSize='1px'; st.left='4px'; st.top='7px';
st.backgroundColor="black"; over.appendChild(view);
                    view=shiftzoom.E('div');
st=view.style; st.height='2px'; st.width='8px';
st.position='absolute'; st.lineHeight='1px';
```

```
      st.fontSize='1px'; st.left='14px'; st.top='7px';
      st.backgroundColor="black"; over.appendChild(view);
                      view=shiftzoom.E('div');
    st=view.style; st.height='8px'; st.width='2px';
    st.position='absolute'; st.lineHeight='1px';
    st.fontSize='1px'; st.left='17px'; st.top='4px';
    st.backgroundColor="black"; over.appendChild(view);
                      view=shiftzoom.E('div');
    st=view.style; st.height='2px'; st.width='8px';
    st.position='absolute'; st.lineHeight='1px';
    st.fontSize='1px'; st.left='30px'; st.top='7px';
    st.backgroundColor="black"; over.appendChild(view);
                      view=shiftzoom.E('div');
    view.id=img.id+'_kbin'; st=view.style;
    st.height=(img.bmode?16:14)+'px'; st.cursor='help';
    st.width=(img.bmode?10:8)+'px'; st.display="block";
                      st.position='absolute';
    st.border=img.bc; st.borderBottom=img.dc;
    st.borderRight=img.dc; st.left='0px'; st.top='0px';
    img.ttipid=img.id+'_ttip';
                      if(img.trident)
    {view.onmouseover=new
    Function('shiftzoom._showTooltip("'+img.id+'");');
    view.onmouseout=new
    Function('shiftzoom._killTooltip("'+img.id+'");');}
                      else
    {view.setAttribute("onmouseover","shiftzoom._showToo
    ltip('"+img.id+"');");
    view.setAttribute("onmouseout","shiftzoom._killToolt
    ip('"+img.id+"');");}
                      over.appendChild(view);
    img.kbinid=view.id; view=shiftzoom.E('div');
    view.id=img.id+'_zoin'; view.title=img.intitle;
    st=view.style; st.height=(img.bmode?16:14)+'px';
    st.width=(img.bmode?16:14)+'px';
                      st.display="block";
    st.position='absolute'; st.border=img.bc;
    st.borderBottom=img.dc; st.borderRight=img.dc;
    st.left='10px';st.top='0px';
                      if(img.trident)
    {view.onclick=new
    Function('shiftzoom._setCursor(this,1,"'+img.id+'");
    ');}else
    {view.setAttribute("onclick","shiftzoom._setCursor(t
    his,1,'"+img.id+"');");}
                      over.appendChild(view);
    img.zoinid=view.id; view=shiftzoom.E('div');
    view.id=img.id+'_zout'; view.title=img.outtitle;
    st=view.style; st.height=(img.bmode?16:14)+'px';
    st.width=(img.bmode?16:14)+'px';
                      st.display="block";
```

STUTTER

```
st.position='absolute'; st.border=img.bc;
st.borderBottom=img.dc; st.borderRight=img.dc;
st.left='26px'; st.top='0px';
                        if(img.trident)
{view.onclick=new
Function('shiftzoom._setCursor(this,0,"'+img.id+'");
');}else
{view.setAttribute("onclick","shiftzoom._setCursor(t
his,0,'"+img.id+"');"); }
                        over.appendChild(view);
img.zoutid=view.id; over=shiftzoom.E('div');
over.id=img.id+'_info'; st=over.style;
st.visibility='hidden'; st.height='16px';
st.width='7em'; st.left=(img.buttons?'42px':'0px');
st.top='0px';
                        st.display="block";
st.overflow='hidden'; st.position='absolute';
st.lineHeight='16px'; st.fontSize='10px';
st.fontFamily='Arial, Helvetica, sans-serif';
                        st.fontStyle='normal';
st.fontWeight='bold'; st.textShadow='0px 0px 4px
black'; st.color="#ffffff"; if(img.trident)
{st.filter="alpha(opacity=100)";}else{st.opacity=1;}
                        st.cursor='default';
div.appendChild(over); img.infoid=over.id;
                        view=shiftzoom.E('div');
st=view.style; st.position='absolute';
st.height='16px'; st.width='7em'; st.left='0px';
st.top='0px';
                        st.display="block";
st.backgroundColor="#000000"; if(img.trident)
{st.filter="alpha(opacity=50)";}else{st.opacity=0.50
;} over.appendChild(view);
                        view=shiftzoom.E('div');
view.id=img.id+'_text'; st=view.style;
st.position='absolute'; st.height='16px';
st.width='7em'; st.left='0px'; st.top='0px';
st.textAlign='center';
                        st.verticalAlign='middle';
st.overflow='hidden'; st.display="block";
st.color="#ffffff"; if(img.trident)
{st.filter="alpha(opacity=100)";}
                        over.appendChild(view);
img.textid=view.id; view.innerHTML="100 /
"+parseInt(img.xfactor*100)+" %";
over=shiftzoom.E('div'); over.id=img.id+'_over';
st=over.style;
st.height=(outer.height*img.ovsfact)+'px';
st.width=(outer.width*img.ovsfact)+'px';
                        st.display="block";
st.position='absolute'; st.bottom='0px';
```

```
st.right='0px'; st.borderLeft=img.ovborder+'px solid
'+img.ovbcolor; st.borderTop=img.ovborder+'px solid
'+img.ovbcolor;
                        if(img.webkit||img.bshadow)
{st.borderLeft='0px solid '+img.ovbcolor;
st.borderTop='0px solid '+img.ovbcolor;
st.boxShadow="0px 0px 8px black";
                        st.WebkitBoxShadow="0px 0px
8px black"; st.MozBoxShadow="0px 0px 8px black";
st.KhtmlBoxShadow="0px 0px 8px black";}
                        st.MozUserSelect="none";
st.KhtmlUserSelect="none"; st.visibility="hidden";
over.unselectable="on"; div.appendChild(over);
                        view=shiftzoom.E('img');
view.id=img.id+'_tumb'; view.src=xref.src;
st=view.style;
st.height=(outer.height*img.ovsfact)+'px';
st.width=(outer.width*img.ovsfact)+'px';
                        st.display="block";
st.position='absolute'; st.bottom='0px';
st.right='0px'; st.msInterpolationMode=img.bicubic;
over.appendChild(view); img.tumbid=view.id;
view.onmousedown=shiftzoom._catchDrag;
                        view=shiftzoom.E('div');
view.id=img.id+'_view'; view.maxleft=0;
view.maxtop=0; st=view.style; st.lineHeight='1px';
st.fontSize='1px'; st.display="block";
st.position='absolute'; st.left='0px'; st.top='0px';
                        st.border='1px solid
'+img.ovacolor;
st.height=parseInt((outer.height*img.ovsfact)-
(img.bmode?0:2))+'px';
st.width=parseInt((outer.width*img.ovsfact)-
(img.bmode?0:2))+'px';

    if(img.trident){st.background="url('"+img.curpa
th+"nop.gif') transparent";
st.filter="alpha(opacity="+img.ovaopac+")";}else{st.
opacity=img.ovaopac/100;}
                        over.appendChild(view);
img.overid=over.id; img.viewid=view.id;
view.onmousedown=shiftzoom._startMove;
img.oncontextmenu=function() {return false;};
img.onmousedown=shiftzoom._catchKey;
img.onmouseover=shiftzoom._catchOver;
img.onmouseout=shiftzoom._catchOut;
                        if(img.showcoords)
{img.onmousemove=(img.pixelcoords?shiftzoom._showCoo
rds:img.percentcoords?shiftzoom._showPercent:shiftzo
om._showLatLon);}
if(img.zoom>0&&img.fading&&img.overview)
```

```
{img.overview=false; img.special=true;}
                    if(img.zoom>0)
{shiftzoom.zooming(img,img.zoom);}
if(img.xpos!=50||img.ypos!=50)
{shiftzoom.moveto(img,img.xpos+'%',img.ypos+'%');}
                    if(img.icons)
{shiftzoom.construct(img,img.icons);} if(img.fading)
{shiftzoom._fadeImage(img.id,0);}
                }else
{ele.parentNode.removeChild(outer);
ele.style.visibility='visible';}
            }else
{ele.style.visibility='visible';}
        } return false;
    },
    remove : function(img,v) {
        if(img&&typeof(img.ctrlid)==="string") {var
ele,obj=img.parentNode.parentNode;
img.onmousedown=null; img.onmousemove=null;
            document.onmousemove=null;
document.onmouseup=null; document.onkeydown=null;
document.onkeyup=null; document.onkeypress=null;
            if(img.gecko)
{window.removeEventListener('DOMMouseScroll',
shiftzoom._catchWheel, false);}else
{window.onmousewheel=null;}
            ele=shiftzoom.G(img.overid); if(ele)
{obj.removeChild(ele);} ele=shiftzoom.G(img.infoid);
if(ele) {obj.removeChild(ele);}
            ele=shiftzoom.G(img.ctrlid); if(ele)
{obj.removeChild(ele);} ele=shiftzoom.G(img.xycoid);
if(ele) {obj.removeChild(ele);}
            ele=shiftzoom.G(img.isrcid); if(ele)
{obj.removeChild(ele);} ele=shiftzoom.E('img');
ele.id=img.id; img.id=""; img.ctrlid=false;
        ele.width=(v?img.maxwidth:img.minwidth);
ele.height=(v?img.maxheight:img.minheight);
ele.style.width=(v?img.maxwidth:img.minwidth)+'px';
    ele.style.height=(v?img.maxheight:img.minheight
)+'px'; ele.style.border="0px none";
ele.style.cursor="default"; ele.src=img.highres;
    obj.style.width=(v?img.maxwidth:img.minwidth)+'
px';
obj.style.height=(v?img.maxheight:img.minheight)+'px
'; obj.removeChild(img.parentNode);
obj.appendChild(ele);
        }return false;
    },
    construct : function(img,v) {
    if(img&&typeof(v)==="object"&&typeof(img.ctrlid
)==="string") {var
```

```
i,d,x,y,w,h,p,q,r,t,g,s,z,m,n,oe,ie,ele;
            for(i=0; i<v.length; i++)
{w=v[i].w||0; h=v[i].h||0; s=v[i].src||0;
q=v[i].noscale||0; d=v[i].id||0; if(d)
{ele=shiftzoom.G(d); }else {ele=false;}
                if(!ele&&w>=8&&h>=8&&s!='')
{x=Math.abs(v[i].x)||0; y=Math.abs(v[i].y)||0;
p=Math.max(Math.min(Math.abs(v[i].pos),9),0)||0;
                       z=v[i].src2||0;
r=v[i].href||0; t=v[i].title||0; g=v[i].target||0;
oe=shiftzoom.E('a'); if(d) {oe.id=d;} if(r)
{oe.href=r;} if(g) {oe.target=g;}
oe.unselectable="on";
                        oe.style.border="0px none";
oe.style.fontSize="0px"; oe.style.lineHeight="0px";
oe.style.margin="0px"; oe.style.padding="0px";
oe.style.textDecoration="none";
                oe.style.mozUserSelect="none";
oe.style.khtmlUserSelect="none";
oe.style.webkitUserSelect="none";
img.appendChild(oe); ie=shiftzoom.E('img');
                       if(img.notrans)
{ie.src=img.curpath+"nop.gif";
ie.style.filter="progid:DXImageTransform.Microsoft.A
lphaImageLoader(src='"+s+"',
sizingMethod='scale')";}else {ie.src=s;}
                       ie.width=w; ie.height=h;
if(t) {ie.title=t;} ie.unselectable="on";
ie.style.position="absolute"; ie.style.margin="0px";
ie.style.padding="0px"; ie.style.border="0px none";
    ie.style.width=q?w+'px':(w/(img.maxwidth/100))+
'%';
ie.style.height=q?h+'px':(h/(img.maxheight/100))+'%'
; n=(img.maxheight/100); m=(img.maxwidth/100); if(q)
{ie.style.top=(y?y/n:0)+'%';
ie.style.left=(x?x/m:0)+'%';}else {
                         if(!p||p==4||p==5||p==6)
{ie.style.top=((y?y/n:0)-
(parseFloat(ie.style.height)/2))+'%';}else
if(p==7||p==8||p==9) {ie.style.top=((y?y/n:0)-
parseFloat(ie.style.height))+'%';}else
if(p==1||p==2||p==3) {ie.style.top=(y?y/n:0)+'%';}
                       if(!p||p==2||p==5||p==8)
{ie.style.left=((x?x/m:0)-
(parseFloat(ie.style.width)/2))+'%';}else
if(p==3||p==6||p==9) {ie.style.left=((x?x/m:0)-
parseFloat(ie.style.width))+'%';}else
if(p==1||p==4||p==7) {ie.style.left=(x?x/m:0)+'%';}}
                ie.style.mozUserSelect="none";
ie.style.khtmlUserSelect="none";
ie.style.webkitUserSelect="none";
```

STUTTER

```
ie.style.msInterpolationMode=img.bicubic;
                        if(z) {ie.first=s;
ie.secnd=z; if(!img.trident)
{ie.setAttribute("onmouseover","this.src=this.secnd;
");
ie.setAttribute("onmouseout","this.src=this.first;")
;}}
                        oe.appendChild(ie);
if(z&&img.trident)
{oe.onmouseover=shiftzoom._switchOver;
oe.onmouseout=shiftzoom._switchOut;}
                    }
                }
        }return false;
    },
    destruct : function(img,v) {
        if(img&&v&&typeof(img.ctrlid)==="string") {
            if(typeof(v)==="string") {var
ele=shiftzoom.G(v); if(ele) {img.removeChild(ele);}}
if(typeof(v)==="boolean") {img.innerHTML="";}
        }return false;
    },
    moveto : function(img,x,y) {
        if(img&&typeof(img.ctrlid)==="string") {
    if(img.parentNode.width>img.minwidth||img.paren
tNode.height>img.minheight) {
                function LFL(m,i,n){var
d=parseFloat(m); if(d>n){d=n;}else if(d<i){d=i;}
return d;}    var
f,h,v,q=parseFloat((img.parentNode.width-
img.minwidth)/(img.maxwidth-img.minwidth));
                if(typeof(x)=="string")
{if(x.match(/^([+-])?\d*([\.])?\d*$/)) {f=(LFL(x,-
180,180)*-1)+180; x=f*(((img.maxwidth-
img.minwidth)*q)/360); h=(0.5-(f/360))*img.minwidth;
x=x-h;}else if(x.match(/^\d*([\.])?\d*([%]){1,1}$/))
{x=((img.maxwidth-
img.minwidth)*q)*(parseFloat(x)/100);}else
{x=0;}}else {x=(x-(img.minwidth/2))*q;}
                if(typeof(y)=="string")
{if(y.match(/^([+-])?\d*([\.])?\d*$/)) {f=(LFL(y,-
90,90)*-1)+90; y=f*(((img.maxheight-
img.minheight)*q)/180); v=(0.5-
(f/180))*img.minheight; y=y-v;}else
if(y.match(/^\d*([\.])?\d*([%]){1,1}$/))
{y=((img.maxheight-
img.minheight)*q)*(parseFloat(y)/100);}else
{y=0;}}else {y=(y-(img.minheight/2))*q;}
        h=Math.max(0,Math.min(img.maxleft,x||0));
v=Math.max(0,Math.min(img.maxtop,y||0));
img.parentNode.style.left=(h*-1)+'px';
```

```
            img.parentNode.style.top=(v*-1)+'px';
            img.parentNode.left=(h*-1); img.parentNode.top=(v*-
1);
                        if(img.overview) {var
view=shiftzoom.G(img.viewid).style;
     view.left=Math.round((Math.abs(parseInt(img.par
entNode.style.left))/(img.parentNode.width/img.minwi
dth))*img.ovsfact)-(img.bmode?2:0)+'px';

     view.top=Math.round((Math.abs(parseInt(img.pare
ntNode.style.top))/(img.parentNode.height/img.minhei
ght))*img.ovsfact)-(img.bmode?2:0)+'px';
                        }
                    }
            }return false;
        },
        zooming : function(img,v) {
            if(img&&typeof(img.ctrlid)==="string") {
                if(typeof(v)==="number") {var
mw,mh,mx,my,f;
v=Math.max(0,Math.min(100,parseFloat(v)));
f=v>0?v/100:0;
                    mw=Math.round(f*(img.maxwidth-
img.minwidth))+img.minwidth;
mh=Math.round(f*(img.maxheight-
img.minheight))+img.minheight;
                    mx=Math.round((mw/2)-
(img.minwidth/2))*-1; my=Math.round((mh/2)-
(img.minheight/2))*-1;
                img.parentNode.style.width=mw+'px';
img.parentNode.style.height=mh+'px';
img.parentNode.style.left=mx+'px';
img.parentNode.style.top=my+'px';
                    img.parentNode.width=mw;
img.parentNode.height=mh; img.parentNode.left=mx;
img.parentNode.top=my;
img.maxleft=img.parentNode.width-img.minwidth;
img.maxtop=img.parentNode.height-img.minheight;
    if(img.parentNode.width>img.minwidth||img.paren
tNode.height>img.minheight) {
                        if(img.trident)
{img.style.cursor="url('"+img.curpath+"grab.cur'),mo
ve";}else {img.style.cursor="move";}
                        if(img.overview)
{shiftzoom._setOverview(img);
shiftzoom.G(img.overid).style.visibility="visible";}
                    }else
{img.style.cursor="crosshair"; if(img.overview)
{shiftzoom.G(img.overid).style.visibility="hidden";}
}
                }
```

```
            }return false;
    },
    kenburns : function(img,obj) {
        if(img&&typeof(img.ctrlid)==="string") {
            function
GNV(v){if(typeof(v)==="number")
{v=Math.max(0,Math.min(100,parseFloat(v)));}else
{v=0.5;} return v;}; var
io=false,x=obj[0],y=obj[1],z=obj[2],p=obj[3]||false,
s=obj[4]||false,d=obj[5]||false,b=obj[6]||false,a=ob
j[7]||false;
            if(typeof(p)==="number") {if(p==3)
{io=true;}else if(p==0) {p=1;}else
{p=Math.max(0,Math.min(2,parseFloat(p)));}}else
{p=1;} if(typeof(s)==="number")
{s=Math.max(10,Math.min(100,parseInt(s)));}
if(typeof(d)==="number")
{d=Math.max(10,Math.min(100,parseInt(d)));}else
{d=30;}
            var
fz,mz,ix,iy,wf,hf,sw,sh,sx,sy,ew,eh,ex,ey; x=GNV(x);
y=GNV(y); z=GNV(z); fz=z*0.01;
if(img.lowres&&img.highres)
{shiftzoom.source(img,img.lowres,false,true);}
img.zoomin=false; img.zoomout=false;
    if(img.parentNode.width>img.minwidth||img.paren
tNode.height>img.minheight) {if(img.trident)
{img.style.cursor="url('"+img.curpath+"grab.cur'),mo
ve";}else {img.style.cursor="move";}}else
{img.style.cursor="crosshair";}
            ix=(img.maxwidth-
img.minwidth)*(x*0.01); iy=(img.maxheight-
img.minheight)*(y*0.01);
sw=parseInt(img.parentNode.style.width);
sh=parseInt(img.parentNode.style.height);
    sx=parseInt(img.parentNode.style.left);
sy=parseInt(img.parentNode.style.top); ew=z>-
1?Math.round(fz*(img.maxwidth-
img.minwidth))+img.minwidth:sw; eh=z>-
1?Math.round(fz*(img.maxheight-
img.minheight))+img.minheight:sh;
            wf=parseFloat((ew-
img.minwidth)/(img.maxwidth-img.minwidth));
hf=parseFloat((eh-img.minheight)/(img.maxheight-
img.minheight)); ex=Math.max(0,Math.min(ew-
img.minwidth,ix*wf))*-1; ey=Math.max(0,Math.min(eh-
img.minheight,iy*hf))*-1;
            if(typeof(s)!=="number")
{mz=Math.abs(Math.abs(ex)-Math.abs(sx));
mz=Math.max(mz,Math.abs(Math.abs(ey)-Math.abs(sy)));
mz=Math.max(mz,Math.abs(Math.abs(ew)-Math.abs(sw)));
```

```
mz=Math.max(mz,Math.abs(Math.abs(eh)-Math.abs(sh)));
s=Math.round(mz/d);}
                if(img.timer)
{window.clearInterval(img.timer);} var
mx,my,mw,mh,q=0,c=0,t=Math.max(5,s),k=1/t;
img.timer=window.setInterval(function() {
                q=io?((-
Math.cos((k*c)*Math.PI)/2)+0.5)||0:Math.pow((k*c),p)
||0; mw=Math.ceil(sw+(q*(ew-sw)));
mh=Math.ceil(sh+(q*(eh-sh)));
mx=Math.ceil(sx+(q*(ex-sx)));
my=Math.ceil(sy+(q*(ey-sy)));
                img.parentNode.style.width=mw+'px';
img.parentNode.style.height=mh+'px';
img.parentNode.style.left=mx+'px';
img.parentNode.style.top=my+'px';
img.parentNode.width=mw; img.parentNode.height=mh;
                img.parentNode.left=mx;
img.parentNode.top=my; if(img.divbug)
{img.parentNode.firstChild.style.width=mw+'px';
img.parentNode.firstChild.style.height=mh+'px';}
                c++; if(c>t)
{window.clearInterval(img.timer);
img.maxleft=img.parentNode.width-img.minwidth;
img.maxtop=img.parentNode.height-img.minheight;
img.zoomin=false; img.zoomout=false;
                if(img.lowres&&img.highres)
{shiftzoom.source(img,img.highres,false,true);}
if(img.parentNode.width>img.minwidth||img.parentNode
.height>img.minheight) {
                        if(img.trident)
{img.style.cursor="url('"+img.curpath+"grab.cur'),mo
ve";}else {img.style.cursor="move";}
if(img.overview) {shiftzoom._setOverview(img);
shiftzoom.G(img.overid).style.visibility="visible";}
                }else
{img.style.cursor="crosshair"; if(img.overview)
{shiftzoom.G(img.overid).style.visibility="hidden";}
}
                    if(img.automode)
{if(b&&typeof(b)==="string"&&eval('typeof
'+b)=="function")
{window.setTimeout("window['"+b+"']('"+(typeof(a)=='
number'||typeof(a)=='string'?a:'')+"')",30);}
    window.setTimeout("shiftzoom._next(shiftzoom.G(
'"+img.id+"'))",img.autowait+1000);}else
{if(b&&typeof(b)==="string"&&eval('typeof
'+b)=="function")
{window.setTimeout("window['"+b+"']('"+(typeof(a)=='
number'||typeof(a)=='string'?a:'')+"')",200);}}}
            },d);
```

STUTTER

```
        }return false;
    },
    play : function(img,d,l,obj,c) {
        if(img&&typeof(img.ctrlid)==="string") {
     if(!img.automode&&typeof(d)==="number"&&typeof(
l)==="boolean"&&typeof(obj)==="object") {
                        if(obj.length>=1) {var n=0,mx=3,i;
for(i=0; i<obj.length; ++i)
{n=Math.max(0,obj[i].length);mx=n<mx?n:mx;}
img.callback=c&&typeof(c)==="string"&&eval('typeof
'+c)=="function"?c:Null;
                        if(mx>=3) {img.step=obj;
img.cpos=0; img.automode=true; img.autoloop=l;
img.autowait=Math.abs(d); img.nozoom=true;
                            if(img.overview)
{shiftzoom.set(img,'overview',false);}
if(img.buttons)
{shiftzoom.set(img,'buttons',false);}
if(img.showcoords)
{shiftzoom.set(img,'showcoords',false);}
shiftzoom.kenburns(shiftzoom.G(img.id),img.step[img.
cpos]);
                        }
                    }
                }
        }return false;
    },
    stop : function(img) {
        if(img&&typeof(img.ctrlid)==="string") {
            if(img.automode) {
                img.automode=false; if(img.timer)
{window.clearInterval(img.timer);}
img.autoloop=false; img.cpos=0;
img.maxleft=img.parentNode.width-img.minwidth;
img.maxtop=img.parentNode.height-img.minheight;
                if(img.lowres&&img.highres)
{shiftzoom.source(img,img.highres,false,true);}
if(img.parentNode.width>img.minwidth||img.parentNode
.height>img.minheight) {
                    if(img.trident)
{img.style.cursor="url('"+img.curpath+"grab.cur'),mo
ve";}else {img.style.cursor="move";}
if(img.overview) {shiftzoom._setOverview(img);
shiftzoom.G(img.overid).style.visibility="visible";}
                }else
{img.style.cursor="crosshair"; if(img.overview)
{shiftzoom.G(img.overid).style.visibility="hidden";}
} if(img.callback)
{window.setTimeout("window['"+img.callback+"']()",20
0);}
            }
```

```
            }return false;
      },
      source : function(img,src,v,z) {
            if(img&&typeof(img.ctrlid)==="string") {

      if(typeof(src)==="string"&&typeof(v)==="boolean
") {
                  var tmp=new Image();
shiftzoom.G(img.xrefid)
                  tmp.onload=function() {
      shiftzoom.G(img.ctrlid).style.visibility="hidde
n";
shiftzoom.G(img.overid).style.visibility="hidden";
shiftzoom.G(img.xycoid).style.visibility="hidden";
                        if(v==true) {

      shiftzoom.G(img.isrcid).src=tmp.src; if(!z)
{if(img.trident) {tmp.onload=''; tmp=null;} delete
tmp;} shiftzoom._fadeOut(img.id,100);
                        }else if(v==false) {var
obj=shiftzoom.G(img.xrefid);
                              obj.src=tmp.src;
obj.style.msInterpolationMode=img.bicubic; if(!z)
{shiftzoom.G(img.tumbid).src=obj.src;
if(img.highres!=obj.src) {img.highres=obj.src;}
if(img.trident) {tmp.onload=''; tmp=null;} delete
tmp;} if(img.buttons)
{shiftzoom.G(img.ctrlid).style.visibility="visible";
}

      if(img.overview&&(img.parentNode.width>img.minw
idth||img.parentNode.height>img.minheight))
{shiftzoom.G(img.overid).style.visibility="visible";
} if(img.showcoords)
{shiftzoom.G(img.xycoid).style.visibility="visible";
}

                        }
                  }; tmp.src=src;
            }
      }return false;
      },
      lowsource : function(img,src) {
            if(img&&typeof(img.ctrlid)==="string") {

      if(typeof(src)==="string"&&!img.automode&&!img.
zoomin&&!img.zoomout) {
                  var low=new Image();
low.onload=function() {img.lowres=low.src;
if(img.trident) {low.onload=''; low=null;} delete
low;}; low.src=src;
            }
```

```
            }return false;
    },
    info : function(img,v) {
         if(img&&typeof(img.ctrlid)==="string") {
              if(v&&typeof(v)==="string")
{img.infoblock=v;}else {img.infoblock=img.defblock;}
         }return false;
    },
    set : function(img,d,v) {
         if(img&&typeof(img.ctrlid)==="string") {
              if(d&&typeof(v)==="boolean") {
                   switch(d.toLowerCase()) {
                        case 'overview':
if(v==false&&img.overview==true)
{shiftzoom.G(img.overid).style.visibility="hidden";}
else if(v==true&&img.overview==false) {

     if(img.parentNode.width>img.minwidth||img.parentNode.height>img.minheight)
{shiftzoom._setOverview(img);
shiftzoom.G(img.overid).style.visibility="visible";}
else
{shiftzoom.G(img.overid).style.visibility="hidden";}
}img.overview=v; break;
                        case 'showcoords':
if(v==false&&img.showcoords==true)
{img.onmousemove=null;
shiftzoom.G(img.xycoid).style.visibility="hidden";}else

     if(v==true&&img.showcoords==false)
{shiftzoom.G(img.xycoid).style.visibility="visible";
img.onmousemove=shiftzoom._showCoords;}img.showcoords=v; break;
                        case 'pixelcoords':
if(v==false&&img.pixelcoords==true&&img.showcoords==true) {img.onmousemove=shiftzoom._showLatLon;}else

     if(v==true&&img.pixelcoords==false&&img.showcoords==true)
{img.onmousemove=shiftzoom._showCoords;}img.pixelcoords=v; break;
                        case 'percentcoords':
if(v==false&&img.percentcoords==true&&img.showcoords==true) {img.onmousemove=shiftzoom._showLatLon;}else

     if(v==true&&img.percentcoords==false&&img.showcoords==true)
{img.onmousemove=shiftzoom._showPercent;}img.percentcoords=v; break;
                        case 'buttons':
```

```
if(v==false&&img.buttons==true)
{shiftzoom.G(img.ctrlid).style.visibility="hidden";
shiftzoom.G(img.infoid).style.left='0px';}else

    if(v==true&&img.buttons==false)
{shiftzoom.G(img.infoid).style.left='42px';
shiftzoom.G(img.ctrlid).style.visibility="visible";}
img.buttons=v; break;
                        case 'zoomin':
if(!img.nozoom&&!img.buttons&&(parseInt(img.parentNo
de.style.width)<img.maxwidth||parseInt(img.parentNod
e.style.height)<img.maxheight)) {
                        if(v==true) {img.zoomin=true;
img.zoomout=false; if(img.gecko)
{img.style.cursor="-moz-zoom-in";}else
if(img.webkit) {img.style.cursor="-webkit-zoom-in";}
                        else if(img.trident)
{img.style.cursor="url('"+img.curpath+"zoom-
in.cur'),crosshair";}else
{img.style.cursor="crosshair";}}else
{img.zoomin=false;}}break;
                        case 'zoomout':
if(!img.nozoom&&!img.buttons&&(parseInt(img.parentNo
de.style.width)>img.minwidth||parseInt(img.parentNod
e.style.height)>img.minheight)) {
                        if(v==true)
{img.zoomout=true; img.zoomin=false; if(img.gecko)
{img.style.cursor="-moz-zoom-out";}else
if(img.webkit) {img.style.cursor="-webkit-zoom-
out";}
                        else if(img.trident)
{img.style.cursor="url('"+img.curpath+"zoom-
out.cur'),crosshair";}else
{img.style.cursor="crosshair";}}else
{img.zoomout=false;}}break;
                        case 'nozoom': img.nozoom=v;
break;
                    }
                }
            }return false;
        },
        get : function(img,d) {
            if(img&&d&&typeof(img.ctrlid)==="string") {
                if(d.toLowerCase()=="maxzoomx")
{return img.xfactor;}else
if(d.toLowerCase()=="maxzoomy") {return
img.yfactor;}else
                if(d.toLowerCase()=="maxwidth")
{return img.maxwidth;}else
if(d.toLowerCase()=="maxheight") {return
img.maxheight;}else
```

STUTTER

```
                if(d.toLowerCase()=="playing") {return
img.automode;}else if(d.toLowerCase()=="currentxyz")
{
                var
q=parseFloat((img.parentNode.width-
img.minwidth)/(img.maxwidth-
img.minwidth)),z=Math.min(Math.max(q*100,0),100)||0;
                var
x=Math.min(Math.max(((Math.abs(parseFloat(img.parent
Node.style.left))/((img.maxwidth-
img.minwidth)*q))*100),0),100)||0;
                var
y=Math.min(Math.max(((Math.abs(parseFloat(img.parent
Node.style.top))/((img.maxheight-
img.minheight)*q))*100),0),100)||0;
                    return {x:x,y:y,z:z};
                }
        }return false;
    },
    G : function(v)
{return(document.getElementById(v));},
    E : function(v)
{return(document.createElement(v));},
    L : function(s,v) {s=s.toUpperCase()||'LOG';
if(window.console) {if(!window.console.warn)
{window.console.log(s+': '+v);}else
{window.console[s.toLowerCase()||'log'](v);}}else
if(window.opera) {opera.postError(s+': '+v);}else
{window.document.title=s+': '+v;} return false;},
    _next : function(img) {
        if(img&&typeof(img.ctrlid)==="string") {
            if(img.automode) {

    if(img.autoloop&&img.cpos<(img.step.length-1))
{img.cpos=img.cpos+1;}else
if(img.autoloop&&img.cpos>=(img.step.length-1))
{img.cpos=0;}else
if(!img.autoloop&&img.cpos<(img.step.length-1))
{img.cpos=img.cpos+1;}else
{img.cpos=img.step.length; }
                if(img.cpos<img.step.length)
{shiftzoom.kenburns(shiftzoom.G(img.id),img.step[img
.cpos]);}else {shiftzoom.stop(img);}
                }
        }return false;
    },
    _setOverview : function(img) {var
view=shiftzoom.G(img.viewid);

    view.style.width=(Math.round((img.ovsfact*img.m
inwidth)/(img.parentNode.width/img.minwidth))-
```

```
(img.bmode?0:2))+'px';

    view.style.height=(Math.round((img.ovsfact*img.
minheight)/(img.parentNode.height/img.minheight))-
(img.bmode?0:2))+'px';

    view.style.left=Math.round((Math.abs(img.parent
Node.left)/(img.parentNode.width/img.minwidth))*img.
ovsfact)-(img.bmode?2:0)+'px';

    view.style.top=Math.round((Math.abs(img.parentN
ode.top)/(img.parentNode.height/img.minheight))*img.
ovsfact)-(img.bmode?2:0)+'px';
        view.maxleft=(img.minwidth*img.ovsfact)-
(img.bmode?0:2)-parseInt(view.style.width);
        view.maxtop=(img.minheight*img.ovsfact)-
(img.bmode?0:2)-parseInt(view.style.height);
        return false;
    },
    _findPosXY : function(ele) {var
t,d={x:ele.offsetLeft, y:ele.offsetTop};
if(ele.offsetParent) {
t=shiftzoom._findPosXY(ele.offsetParent); d.x+=t.x;
d.y+=t.y;} return d;},
    _getMousePos : function (ex,ey,px,py) {var
ox,oy,k={ox:0,oy:0,ex:ex,ey:ey };
        if(self.pageXOffset||self.pageYOffset)
{ox=self.pageXOffset; if(ox>0&&px==ex) {ex-=ox;}
oy=self.pageYOffset; if(oy>0&&py==ey) {ey-=oy;}}else
        if(document.documentElement)
{ox=document.documentElement.scrollLeft;
oy=document.documentElement.scrollTop;}else
        if(document.body)
{ox=document.body.scrollLeft;
oy=document.body.scrollTop;} k.ox=ox; k.oy=oy;
k.ex=ex; k.ey=ey; return k;
    },
    _showCoords : function(e) {
        if(cvi_szactive!=null) {var
k,t,x,y,ex,ey,px=0,py=0,o=shiftzoom.G(cvi_szactive),
w=o.parentNode.width,h=o.parentNode.height;
            e=e?e:window.event; ex=e.clientX;
ey=e.clientY; if(e.pageX||e.pageY) {px=e.pageX;
py=e.pageY;} k=shiftzoom._getMousePos(ex,ey,px,py);
            t=shiftzoom._findPosXY(o);
x=Math.min(Math.max(k.ex+k.ox-t.x,0),w);
y=Math.min(Math.max(k.ey+k.oy-t.y,0),h);

    shiftzoom.G(o.cposid).innerHTML='<span>x:'+x+'
y:'+y+'<\/span>';
        }return false;
```

```
        },
        _showPercent : function(e) {
            if(cvi_szactive!=null) {var
k,t,x,y,z,ex,ey,px=0,py=0,na=!Number.prototype.toFix
ed?0:1,o=shiftzoom.G(cvi_szactive),w=o.parentNode.wi
dth,h=o.parentNode.height;
            e=e?e:window.event; ex=e.clientX;
ey=e.clientY; if(e.pageX||e.pageY) {px=e.pageX;
py=e.pageY;} k=shiftzoom._getMousePos(ex,ey,px,py);
t=shiftzoom._findPosXY(o);

    x=parseFloat((Math.min(Math.max(k.ex+k.ox-
t.x,0.0),w)/w)*100); x=na?x.toFixed(2):parseInt(x);
y=parseFloat((Math.min(Math.max(k.ey+k.oy-
t.y,0.0),h)/h)*100);
            y=na?y.toFixed(2):parseInt(y);
z=parseFloat(((w-o.minwidth)/(o.maxwidth-
o.minwidth))*100); z=na?z.toFixed(2):parseInt(z);

    shiftzoom.G(o.cposid).innerHTML='<span>x:'+x+'%
y:'+y+'% z:'+z+'%<\/span>';
        }return false;
        },
        _showLatLon : function(e) {
            if(cvi_szactive!=null) {function
parseDMS(v,n){var d,m,s; d=parseInt(v);
m=Math.abs(parseFloat(v-d)*60);
s=Math.abs(parseFloat(parseInt(m)-m)*60); return
Math.abs(d)+"°"+parseInt(m)+"'"+parseInt(s)+"''
"+n;}
            var
k,t,x,y,lat,lon,ex,ey,px=0,py=0,o=document.getElemen
tById(cvi_szactive),w=o.parentNode.width,h=o.parentN
ode.height;
            e=e?e:window.event; ex=e.clientX;
ey=e.clientY; if(e.pageX||e.pageY) {px=e.pageX;
py=e.pageY;} k=shiftzoom._getMousePos(ex,ey,px,py);
            t=shiftzoom._findPosXY(o);
x=Math.min(Math.max(k.ex+k.ox-t.x,0),w);
y=Math.min(Math.max(k.ey+k.oy-t.y,0),h);
            lon=(x*360/w)-180; lat=90-(y*180/h);
lon=parseDMS(lon,lon!=0?(lon<0?"W":"E"):"");
lat=parseDMS(lat,lat!=0?(lat<0?"S":"N"):"");

    shiftzoom.G(o.cposid).innerHTML='<span>Lat:
'+lat+' &bull; Lon: '+lon+'<\/span>';
        }return false;
        },
        _killTooltip : function(id) {var
ison,img=shiftzoom.G(id);
ison=shiftzoom.G(img.ttipid); if(ison)
```

```
{document.getElementsByTagName("body")[0].removeChil
d(ison);}return false;},
    _showTooltip : function(id) {var
ison,over,view,img=shiftzoom.G(id);
ison=shiftzoom.G(img.ttipid);
        if(!ison) {var
t=shiftzoom._findPosXY(img.parentNode.parentNode);
over=shiftzoom.E('div'); if(img.trident)
{over.style.backgroundColor='black';}
            over.id=img.ttipid;
over.style.height='auto'; over.style.width='auto';
over.style.display='block';
over.style.position='absolute';
over.style.filter="alpha(opacity=0)";
            over.style.opacity=0;
over.style.left=(t.x+10)+'px';
over.style.top=t.y+'px';
over.style.visibility='visible';
over.style.border='solid 2px white';
            over.style.borderRadius='6px';
over.style.MozBorderRadius='6px';
over.style.KhtmlBorderRadius='6px';
over.style.WebkitBorderRadius='6px';
            over.style.boxShadow='0px 0px 8px
black'; over.style.MozBoxShadow='0px 0px 8px black';
over.style.WebkitBoxShadow='0px 0px 8px black';
over.style.KhtmlBoxShadow='0px 0px 8px black';
            over.style.MozUserSelect="none";
over.style.KhtmlUserSelect="none";
over.unselectable="on";
document.getElementsByTagName("body")[0].appendChild
(over);
            if(!img.trident)
{view=shiftzoom.E('div'); view.style.height='100%';
view.style.width='100%'; view.style.left='0px';
view.style.top='0px';
view.style.position='absolute';
view.style.opacity=0.5;
            view.style.backgroundColor='black';
view.style.borderRadius='4px';
view.style.MozBorderRadius='4px';
view.style.KhtmlBorderRadius='4px';
view.style.WebkitBorderRadius='4px';
over.appendChild(view);}
            view=shiftzoom.E('div');
view.style.display='block'; view.style.left='0px';
view.style.top='0px';
view.style.position='relative';
            view.style.textAlign='left';
view.style.verticalAlign='middle';
view.style.color='white';
```

STUTTER

```
view.style.fontSize='12px';
view.style.fontFamily='Arial,Helvetica,sans-serif';
            view.style.fontStyle='normal';
view.style.fontWeight='bold';
view.style.whiteSpace='nowrap';
view.style.textShadow='black 0px 0px 4px';
view.style.margin='10px';
            view.innerHTML=img.infoblock;
over.appendChild(view); if(img.timer)
{window.clearInterval(img.timer);} var
q=0,c=0,t=5,k=20;

    img.timer=window.setInterval(function() {q+=k;
over.style.filter="alpha(opacity="+q+")";
over.style.opacity=q/100;  c++;
                if(c>t)
{window.clearInterval(img.timer);
over.style.filter="alpha(opacity=100)";
over.style.opacity=1;}
            },30);
        }return false;
    },
    _setCursor : function(ele,d,id) {var
img=shiftzoom.G(id);
        if(!img.nozoom) {var
butt=shiftzoom.G(d==1?img.zoutid:img.zoinid).style;
img.zoomin=false; img.zoomout=false;
            ele.style.border=img.bc;
ele.style.borderBottom=img.dc;
ele.style.borderRight=img.dc;
                butt.border=img.bc;
butt.borderBottom=img.dc; butt.borderRight=img.dc;

    if(d==1&&(parseInt(img.parentNode.style.width)<
img.maxwidth||parseInt(img.parentNode.style.height)<
img.maxheight)) {
                    ele.style.border=img.bc;
ele.style.borderTop=img.dc;
ele.style.borderLeft=img.dc; img.zoomin=true;
                    if(img.gecko) {img.style.cursor="-
moz-zoom-in";}else if(img.webkit)
{img.style.cursor="-webkit-zoom-in";}
                    else if(img.trident)
{img.style.cursor="url('"+img.curpath+"zoom-
in.cur'),crosshair";}else
{img.style.cursor="crosshair";}
                }else
if(d==0&&(parseInt(img.parentNode.style.width)>img.m
inwidth||parseInt(img.parentNode.style.height)>img.m
inheight)) {
                    ele.style.border=img.bc;
```

```
ele.style.borderTop=img.dc;
ele.style.borderLeft=img.dc; img.zoomout=true;
                if(img.gecko) {img.style.cursor="-
moz-zoom-out";}else if(img.webkit)
{img.style.cursor="-webkit-zoom-out";}
                else if(img.trident)
{img.style.cursor="url('"+img.curpath+"zoom-
out.cur'),crosshair";}else
{img.style.cursor="crosshair";}
            }else {img.style.cursor=img.pointer;}
        }return false;
    },
    _zoomIn :
function(id,ct,st,sw,ew,sh,eh,sx,ex,sy,ey,nz) {
        if(!nz) {var
mw,mh,mx,my,obj=shiftzoom.G(id);

    if(parseInt(obj.parentNode.style.width)<obj.max
width||parseInt(obj.parentNode.style.height)<obj.max
height) {clearInterval(cvi_sztimer);

    mw=Math.max(obj.minwidth,Math.min(obj.maxwidth,
Math.round(ew*ct/st+sw)));
mx=Math.round(ex*ct/st+sx);

    mh=Math.max(obj.minheight,Math.min(obj.maxheigh
t,Math.round(eh*ct/st+sh)));
my=Math.round(ey*ct/st+sy);

    obj.parentNode.style.width=mw+'px';
obj.parentNode.style.height=mh+'px';
obj.parentNode.style.left=mx+'px';
obj.parentNode.style.top=my+'px'; ct++;
                if(obj.divbug)
{obj.parentNode.firstChild.style.width=mw+'px';
obj.parentNode.firstChild.style.height=mh+'px';}

    shiftzoom.G(obj.textid).innerHTML=parseInt((mw/
obj.minwidth)*100)+" / "+parseInt(obj.xfactor*100)+"
%";

    cvi_sztimer=setInterval("shiftzoom._zoomIn('"+i
d+"',"+ct+","+st+","+sw+","+ew+","+sh+","+eh+","+sx+
","+ex+","+sy+","+ey+","+nz+")",obj.millisec);
            }else {clearInterval(cvi_sztimer); }
        }return false;
    },
    _zoomOut :
function(id,rm,ct,st,sw,ew,sh,eh,sx,ex,sy,ey,nz) {
        if(!nz) {var
mw,mh,mx,my,obj=shiftzoom.G(id);
```

STUTTER

```
    if(parseInt(obj.parentNode.style.width)>obj.min
width||parseInt(obj.parentNode.style.height)>obj.min
height) {clearInterval(cvi_sztimer);

    mw=Math.max(obj.minwidth,Math.min(obj.maxwidth,
Math.round(ew*ct/st+sw)));
mx=Math.round(ex*ct/st+sx);

    mh=Math.max(obj.minheight,Math.min(obj.maxheigh
t,Math.round(eh*ct/st+sh)));
my=Math.round(ey*ct/st+sy);

    obj.parentNode.style.width=mw+'px';
obj.parentNode.style.height=mh+'px';
obj.parentNode.style.left=mx+'px';
obj.parentNode.style.top=my+'px'; ct++;
                if(obj.divbug)
{obj.parentNode.firstChild.style.width=mw+'px';
obj.parentNode.firstChild.style.height=mh+'px';}

    shiftzoom.G(obj.textid).innerHTML=parseInt((mw/
obj.minwidth)*100)+" / "+parseInt(obj.xfactor*100)+"
%";

    cvi_sztimer=setInterval("shiftzoom._zoomOut('"+
id+"',"+rm+","+ct+","+st+","+sw+","+ew+","+sh+","+eh
+","+sx+","+ex+","+sy+","+ey+","+nz+")",obj.millisec
);
            }else {clearInterval(cvi_sztimer);
if(obj.webkit&&rm){shiftzoom._stopZoom();}}
        }return false;
    },
    _stopZoom : function() {
        var view, butt, img=shiftzoom._shiftzoom;
document.onmouseup=null;
        clearInterval(cvi_sztimer);
img.zoomin=false; img.zoomout=false;

    img.parentNode.left=parseInt(img.parentNode.sty
le.left);
img.parentNode.top=parseInt(img.parentNode.style.top
);

    img.parentNode.width=parseInt(img.parentNode.st
yle.width);
img.parentNode.height=parseInt(img.parentNode.style.
height);
        img.maxleft=img.parentNode.width-
img.minwidth; img.maxtop=img.parentNode.height-
img.minheight;
```

```
        if(img.parentNode.width>img.minwidth||img.paren
tNode.height>img.minheight) {
                if(img.trident)
{img.style.cursor="url('"+img.curpath+"grab.cur'),mo
ve";}else {img.style.cursor="move";}
                if(img.overview)
{shiftzoom._setOverview(img);
shiftzoom.G(img.overid).style.visibility="visible";}
          }else {img.style.cursor="crosshair";
if(img.overview)
{shiftzoom.G(img.overid).style.visibility="hidden";}
}
          butt=shiftzoom.G(img.zoinid).style;
butt.border=img.bc; butt.borderBottom=img.dc;
butt.borderRight=img.dc;
          butt=shiftzoom.G(img.zoutid).style;
butt.border=img.bc; butt.borderBottom=img.dc;
butt.borderRight=img.dc;
          img.pointer=img.style.cursor;
shiftzoom.G(img.textid).innerHTML=parseInt((img.pare
ntNode.width/img.minwidth)*100)+" /
"+parseInt(img.xfactor*100)+" %";
          if(img.lowres&&img.highres)
{shiftzoom.source(img,img.highres,false,true);}

     cvi_sztimer=setInterval("shiftzoom._fadeInfo('"
+img.id+"',100)",30); shiftzoom._shiftzoom=null;
return false;
     },
     _catchDrag : function(e) {return false; },
     _catchWheel : function(e){
          var d,v=0; e=e?e:window.event;
if(e.wheelDelta) {v=e.wheelDelta/120;
d=(v<0?1:0);}else if (e.detail) {v=-e.detail/3;
d=(v<0?1:0);}
          if(e.preventDefault)
{e.preventDefault();}else {e.returnValue=false;}
if(cvi_szactive!=null&&v!=0) {cvi_szimage=true;
shiftzoom._initZoom(d,(d==1?2:1),true);} return
false;
     },
     _catchOver : function(e) {
          cvi_szactive=this.id; self.focus();
if(this.gecko)
{window.addEventListener('DOMMouseScroll',
shiftzoom._catchWheel, false);}else
{window.onmousewheel=document.onmousewheel=shiftzoom
._catchWheel;} document.onkeyup=shiftzoom._upKey;
document.onkeypress=shiftzoom._pressKey;
document.onkeydown=shiftzoom._downKey; return false;
```

STUTTER

```
    },
    _catchOut : function() {
        cvi_szactive=null; if(this.gecko)
{window.removeEventListener('DOMMouseScroll',
shiftzoom._catchWheel, false);}else
{window.onmousewheel=document.onmousewheel=null;}
document.onkeydown=null; document.onkeypress=null;
document.onkeyup=null; return false;
    },
    _switchOver : function(e) {
        if(window.XMLHttpRequest)
{this.firstChild.src=this.firstChild.secnd; return
false;} else
{this.firstChild.style.filter="progid:DXImageTransfo
rm.Microsoft.AlphaImageLoader(src='"+this.firstChild
.secnd+"', sizingMethod='scale')";} return false;
    },
    _switchOut : function(e) {
        if(window.XMLHttpRequest)
{this.firstChild.src=this.firstChild.first; return
false;} else
{this.firstChild.style.filter="progid:DXImageTransfo
rm.Microsoft.AlphaImageLoader(src='"+this.firstChild
.first+"', sizingMethod='scale')";} return false;
    },
    _catchKey : function(e) {
clearInterval(cvi_sztimer);
        var img=shiftzoom._shiftzoom=this; var
rm=false,mm=false,k,t,ex,ey,px=0,py=0,obj=shiftzoom.
G(img.infoid).style;
        e=e?e:window.event; if(e.which)
{mm=(e.which==2); rm=(e.which==3);}else if(e.button)
{mm=(e.button==4); rm=(e.button==2);}
        if(img.trident)
{obj.filter="alpha(opacity=100)";}else
{obj.opacity=1;} obj.visibility='hidden';
        ex=e.clientX; ey=e.clientY;
if(e.pageX||e.pageY) {px=e.pageX; py=e.pageY;}
k=shiftzoom._getMousePos(ex,ey,px,py);
t=shiftzoom._findPosXY(img.parentNode.parentNode);
        img.mouseX=Math.min(Math.max(k.ex+k.ox-
t.x,0),img.minwidth);
img.mouseY=Math.min(Math.max(k.ey+k.oy-
t.y,0),img.minheight);

    if(((e.altKey&&!e.shiftKey)||rm||img.zoomout)&&
!img.automode&&!img.nozoom&&(img.parentNode.width>im
g.minwidth||img.parentNode.height>img.minheight)) {
            var butt,sw,ew,sh,eh,sx,ex,sy,ey,st;
if(img.gecko) {img.style.cursor="-moz-zoom-
out";}else if(img.webkit) {img.style.cursor="-
```

51

```
webkit-zoom-out";}
                else if(img.trident)
{img.style.cursor="url('"+img.curpath+"zoom-
out.cur'),crosshair";}else
{img.style.cursor="crosshair";}img.pointer=img.style
.cursor;
                if(!img.zoomout)
{butt=shiftzoom.G(img.zoutid).style;
butt.border=img.bc; butt.borderLeft=img.dc;
butt.borderTop=img.dc; img.zoomout=true;}
                sw=img.parentNode.width;
ew=(img.parentNode.width-img.minwidth)*-1;
sh=img.parentNode.height; eh=(img.parentNode.height-
img.minheight)*-1;
sx=parseInt(img.parentNode.style.left); ex=sx*-1;
sy=parseInt(img.parentNode.style.top); ey=sy*-1;

     st=Math.max(1,Math.round((img.parentNode.width/
img.minwidth)*3));
document.onmouseup=shiftzoom._stopZoom;
obj.visibility='visible';
                if(img.lowres&&img.highres)
{shiftzoom.source(img,img.lowres,false,true);}

     cvi_sztimer=setInterval("shiftzoom._zoomOut('"+
img.id+"',"+rm+","+(img.webkit&&rm?1:0)+","+st+","+s
w+","+ew+","+sh+","+eh+","+sx+","+ex+","+sy+","+ey+"
,"+img.nozoom+")",img.millisec);
            }else
if(((!e.altKey&&e.shiftKey)||mm||img.zoomin)&&!img.a
utomode&&!img.nozoom&&(img.parentNode.width<img.maxw
idth||img.parentNode.height<img.maxheight))  {
            var butt,sw,ew,sh,eh,sx,ex,sy,ey,st;
if(img.gecko) {img.style.cursor="-moz-zoom-in";}else
if(img.webkit) {img.style.cursor="-webkit-zoom-in";}
                else if(img.trident)
{img.style.cursor="url('"+img.curpath+"zoom-
in.cur'),crosshair";}else
{img.style.cursor="crosshair";}img.pointer=img.style
.cursor;
                if(!img.zoomin)
{butt=shiftzoom.G(img.zoinid).style;
butt.border=img.bc; butt.borderLeft=img.dc;
butt.borderTop=img.dc; img.zoomin=true;}
                sw=img.parentNode.width;
ew=img.maxwidth-img.parentNode.width;
sh=img.parentNode.height; eh=img.maxheight-
img.parentNode.height;
sx=parseInt(img.parentNode.style.left);
sy=parseInt(img.parentNode.style.top);
```

STUTTER

```
    ex=Math.max(0,Math.min(ew,Math.round(((img.mous
eX-sx)*(img.maxwidth/img.parentNode.width))-
(img.minwidth*0.5)+sx)))*-1;

    ey=Math.max(0,Math.min(eh,Math.round(((img.mous
eY-sy)*(img.maxheight/img.parentNode.height))-
(img.minheight*0.5)+sy)))*-1;

    st=Math.max(1,Math.round((img.maxwidth/img.pare
ntNode.width)*3));
document.onmouseup=shiftzoom._stopZoom;
obj.visibility='visible';
            if(img.lowres&&img.highres)
{shiftzoom.source(img,img.lowres,false,true);}

    cvi_sztimer=setInterval("shiftzoom._zoomIn('"+i
mg.id+"',0,"+st+","+sw+","+ew+","+sh+","+eh+","+sx+"
,"+ex+","+sy+","+ey+","+img.nozoom+")",img.millisec)
;
        }else
if(img.parentNode.width>img.minwidth||img.parentNode
.height>img.minheight) { if(img.automode)
{shiftzoom.stop(img);}
            if(img.gecko) {img.style.cursor="-moz-
grabbing";}else if(img.trident)
{img.style.cursor="url('"+img.curpath+"grabbing.cur'
),move";}else {img.style.cursor="move";}
            var
x=parseInt(img.parentNode.style.left),
y=parseInt(img.parentNode.style.top);
img.mouseX=e.clientX; img.mouseY=e.clientY;

    document.onmousemove=shiftzoom._whilePan;
document.onmouseup=shiftzoom._stopPan;
        }return false;
    },
    _downKey : function(e) {
        if(cvi_szactive!=null) {
            e=e?e:window.event; var
k=(e.keyCode?e.keyCode:e.which),s=e.shiftKey,a=e.alt
Key,w=false,AL=37,AU=38,AR=39,AD=40,HO=36,EN=35,PD=3
4,PU=33,PL=187,MN=189;
            switch(k) {
                case AL : cvi_szimage=true;
shiftzoom._panKey(8,0,s,a); break;
                case AR : cvi_szimage=true;
shiftzoom._panKey(-8,0,s,a); break;
                case AU : cvi_szimage=true;
shiftzoom._panKey(0,8,s,a); break;
                case AD : cvi_szimage=true;
shiftzoom._panKey(0,-8,s,a); break;
```

```
                    case HO : if(cvi_szimage==null)
{cvi_szimage=true; shiftzoom._initZoom(0,1,w);
}break;
                    case EN : if(cvi_szimage==null)
{cvi_szimage=true; shiftzoom._initZoom(1,1,w);
}break;
                    case MN : case PU :
if(cvi_szimage==null) {cvi_szimage=true;
shiftzoom._initZoom(0,4,w); }break;
                    case PL : case PD :
if(cvi_szimage==null) {cvi_szimage=true;
shiftzoom._initZoom(1,4,w); }break;
                }
            }return false;
    },
    _pressKey : function(e) {return false; },
    _upKey : function() {if(cvi_szactive!=null)
{cvi_szimage=null;}return false;},
    _initZoom : function(d,v,w) {var
sw,ew,sh,eh,sx,ex,sy,ey,st,img=shiftzoom.G(cvi_szact
ive);
        if(img.automode) {shiftzoom.stop(img);}

    if(d==0&&!img.nozoom&&(parseInt(img.parentNode.
style.width)>img.minwidth||parseInt(img.parentNode.s
tyle.height)>img.minheight)) {
            if(img.gecko) {img.style.cursor="-moz-
zoom-out";}else if(img.webkit) {img.style.cursor="-
webkit-zoom-out";}
            else if(img.trident)
{img.style.cursor="url('"+img.curpath+"zoom-
out.cur'),crosshair";}else
{img.style.cursor="crosshair";}img.pointer=img.style
.cursor;
            sw=img.parentNode.width;
ew=(img.parentNode.width-img.minwidth)*-1;
sh=img.parentNode.height; eh=(img.parentNode.height-
img.minheight)*-1;

    sx=parseInt(img.parentNode.style.left); ex=sx*-
1; sy=parseInt(img.parentNode.style.top); ey=sy*-1;

    st=Math.max(1,Math.round((img.parentNode.width/
img.minwidth)*v));
            if(img.lowres&&img.highres)
{shiftzoom.source(img,img.lowres,false,true);}

    shiftzoom._zoomKey(d,(w?1:0),w,st,sw,ew,sh,eh,s
x,ex,sy,ey,img.nozoom);
        }else
if(d==1&&!img.nozoom&&(parseInt(img.parentNode.style
```

STUTTER

```
.width)<img.maxwidth||parseInt(img.parentNode.style.
height)<img.maxheight)) {
                if(img.gecko) {img.style.cursor="-moz-
zoom-in";}else if(img.webkit) {img.style.cursor="-
webkit-zoom-in";}
                else if(img.trident)
{img.style.cursor="url('"+img.curpath+"zoom-
in.cur'),crosshair";}else
{img.style.cursor="crosshair";}img.pointer=img.style
.cursor;
                sw=img.parentNode.width;
ew=img.maxwidth-img.parentNode.width;
sh=img.parentNode.height; eh=img.maxheight-
img.parentNode.height;
sx=parseInt(img.parentNode.style.left);
sy=parseInt(img.parentNode.style.top);

    ex=Math.max(0,Math.min(ew,Math.round((((img.min
width/2)-sx)*(img.maxwidth/img.parentNode.width))-
(img.minwidth*0.5)+sx)))*-1;

    ey=Math.max(0,Math.min(eh,Math.round((((img.min
height/2)-
sy)*(img.maxheight/img.parentNode.height))-
(img.minheight*0.5)+sy)))*-1;

    st=Math.max(1,Math.round((img.maxwidth/img.pare
ntNode.width)*v));
                if(img.lowres&&img.highres)
{shiftzoom.source(img,img.lowres,false,true);}

    shiftzoom._zoomKey(d,(w?1:0),w,st,sw,ew,sh,eh,s
x,ex,sy,ey,img.nozoom);
        }return false;
    },
    _zoomKey :
function(d,ct,ww,st,sw,ew,sh,eh,sx,ex,sy,ey,nz) {
        if(cvi_szactive!=null&&!nz) {var
view,mw,mh,mx,my,img=shiftzoom.G(cvi_szactive);

    if(!img.automode&&!img.zoomout&&!img.zoomin) {
                function setoverview() {
                    if(img.lowres&&img.highres)
{shiftzoom.source(img,img.highres,false,true);}

    if(img.parentNode.width>img.minwidth||img.paren
tNode.height>img.minheight) {
                        if(img.trident)
{img.style.cursor="url('"+img.curpath+"grab.cur'),mo
ve";}else {img.style.cursor="move";}
                        if(img.overview)
```

```
{shiftzoom._setOverview(img);
shiftzoom.G(img.overid).style.visibility="visible";}
                   }else
{img.style.cursor="crosshair"; if(img.overview)
{shiftzoom.G(img.overid).style.visibility="hidden";}
}

                         img.pointer=img.style.cursor;
shiftzoom.G(img.infoid).style.visibility='hidden';
                }

     if(d==0&&(parseInt(img.parentNode.style.width)>
img.minwidth||parseInt(img.parentNode.style.height)>
img.minheight)) {

     mw=Math.max(img.minwidth,Math.min(img.maxwidth,
Math.round(ew*ct/st+sw)));
mx=Math.round(ex*ct/st+sx);
mh=Math.max(img.minheight,Math.min(img.maxheight,Mat
h.round(eh*ct/st+sh))); my=Math.round(ey*ct/st+sy);

     shiftzoom.G(img.infoid).style.visibility='visib
le';
shiftzoom.G(img.textid).innerHTML=parseInt((mw/img.m
inwidth)*100)+" / "+parseInt(img.xfactor*100)+" %";

     img.parentNode.style.width=mw+'px';
img.parentNode.style.height=mh+'px';
img.parentNode.style.left=mx+'px';
img.parentNode.style.top=my+'px';
img.parentNode.width=mw; img.parentNode.height=mh;
img.parentNode.left=mx; img.parentNode.top=my;

     img.maxleft=img.parentNode.width-img.minwidth;
img.maxtop=img.parentNode.height-img.minheight;
ct++; if(img.divbug)
{img.parentNode.firstChild.style.width=mw+'px';
img.parentNode.firstChild.style.height=mh+'px';}

     if((cvi_szimage||ww)&&(img.parentNode.width>img
.minwidth||img.parentNode.height>img.minheight)) {
                         if(!ww)
{setTimeout("shiftzoom._zoomKey("+d+","+ct+","+ww+",
"+st+","+sw+","+ew+","+sh+","+eh+","+sx+","+ex+","+s
y+","+ey+","+nz+")",50);}
                         else {setoverview();
if(cvi_szactive!=null) {cvi_szimage=null;}}
                }else {setoverview();}
           }else
if(d==1&&(parseInt(img.parentNode.style.width)<img.m
axwidth||parseInt(img.parentNode.style.height)<img.m
axheight)) {
```

STUTTER

```
    mw=Math.max(img.minwidth,Math.min(img.maxwidth,
Math.round(ew*ct/st+sw)));
mx=Math.round(ex*ct/st+sx);
mh=Math.max(img.minheight,Math.min(img.maxheight,Mat
h.round(eh*ct/st+sh)));  my=Math.round(ey*ct/st+sy);

    shiftzoom.G(img.infoid).style.visibility='visib
le';
shiftzoom.G(img.textid).innerHTML=parseInt((mw/img.m
inwidth)*100)+" / "+parseInt(img.xfactor*100)+" %";

    img.parentNode.style.width=mw+'px';
img.parentNode.style.height=mh+'px';
img.parentNode.style.left=mx+'px';
img.parentNode.style.top=my+'px';
img.parentNode.width=mw; img.parentNode.height=mh;
img.parentNode.left=mx; img.parentNode.top=my;

    img.maxleft=img.parentNode.width-img.minwidth;
img.maxtop=img.parentNode.height-img.minheight;
ct++; if(img.divbug)
{img.parentNode.firstChild.style.width=mw+'px';
img.parentNode.firstChild.style.height=mh+'px';}

    if((cvi_szimage||ww)&&(img.parentNode.width<img
.maxwidth||img.parentNode.height<img.maxheight)) {
                        if(!ww)
{setTimeout("shiftzoom._zoomKey("+d+","+ct+","+ww+",
"+st+","+sw+","+ew+","+sh+","+eh+","+sx+","+ex+","+s
y+","+ey+","+nz+")",50);}
                        else {setoverview();
if(cvi_szactive!=null) {cvi_szimage=null;}}
                }else {setoverview();}
            }else {setoverview();}
        }
    }return false;
    },
    _panKey : function(h,v,s,a) {
        if(cvi_szactive!=null) {var
img=shiftzoom.G(cvi_szactive); if(img.automode)
{shiftzoom.stop(img);}

    if(!img.automode&&(img.parentNode.width>img.min
width||img.parentNode.height>img.minheight)) {
            var
x=Math.max(0,Math.min(img.maxleft,Math.abs(parseInt(
img.parentNode.style.left))-(s?4*h:a?h/4:h)));
            var
y=Math.max(0,Math.min(img.maxtop,Math.abs(parseInt(i
mg.parentNode.style.top))-(s?4*v:a?v/4:v)));
```

```
                    img.parentNode.style.left=(x*-
1)+'px'; img.parentNode.style.top=(y*-1)+'px';
img.parentNode.left=(x*-1); img.parentNode.top=(y*-
1);
                    if(img.overview) {var
view=shiftzoom.G(img.viewid).style;
      view.left=Math.round((Math.abs(parseInt(img.par
entNode.style.left))/(img.parentNode.width/img.minwi
dth))*img.ovsfact)-(img.bmode?2:0)+'px';
      view.top=Math.round((Math.abs(parseInt(img.pare
ntNode.style.top))/(img.parentNode.height/img.minhei
ght))*img.ovsfact)-(img.bmode?2:0)+'px';
                    } if(cvi_szimage)
{setTimeout("shiftzoom._panKey("+h+","+v+","+s+","+a
+")",50);}
                }
            }return false;
        },
      _fadeImage : function(id,o) {var
img=shiftzoom.G(id);
            if(o<=100) {if(img.trident)
{img.parentNode.style.filter="alpha(opacity="+o+")";
}else {img.parentNode.style.opacity=o/100;} o+=10;
      window.setTimeout("shiftzoom._fadeImage('"+id+"
',"+o+")",30);}else {if(img.buttons)
{shiftzoom.G(img.ctrlid).style.visibility='visible';
} if(img.showcoords)
{shiftzoom.G(img.xycoid).style.visibility='visible';
}
      if(img.special&&(img.parentNode.width>img.minwi
dth||img.parentNode.height>img.minheight))
{img.overview=true; img.special=false;
shiftzoom._setOverview(img);
shiftzoom.G(img.overid).style.visibility="visible";}
            }return false;       },
      _fadeInfo : function(id,o) {
            clearInterval(cvi_sztimer); var
img=shiftzoom.G(id), obj=shiftzoom.G(img.infoid);
if(o>0&&cvi_szactive==img.id&&!img.zoomin&&!img.zoom
out){if(img.trident)
{obj.style.filter="alpha(opacity="+o+")";}else
{obj.style.opacity=o/100;} o-=5;
cvi_sztimer=setInterval("shiftzoom._fadeInfo('"+id+"
',"+o+")",50);}else {if(img.trident)
{obj.style.filter="alpha(opacity=100)";}else
{obj.style.opacity=1;}
obj.style.visibility='hidden';}
            return false; },    _fadeOut : function(id,o)
{
            var img=shiftzoom.G(id); if(o>0)
{if(img.trident){img.parentNode.style.filter="alpha(
```

```
opacity="+o+")";}else
{img.parentNode.style.opacity=o/100;} o-=10;
    window.setTimeout("shiftzoom._fadeOut('"+id+"',
"+o+")",30);}else {var obj=shiftzoom.G(img.xrefid);
obj.src=shiftzoom.G(img.isrcid).src;
shiftzoom.G(img.tumbid).src=obj.src;
        obj.style.msInterpolationMode=img.bicubic;
shiftzoom.G(img.isrcid).src=img.trident?null:null;
if(img.highres!=obj.src) {img.highres=obj.src;}
shiftzoom._fadeIn(id,0);}
        return false;
    },_fadeIn : function(id,o) {var
img=shiftzoom.G(id);
        if(o<=100) {if(img.trident)
{img.parentNode.style.filter="alpha(opacity="+o+")";
}else {img.parentNode.style.opacity=o/100;} o+=10;
    window.setTimeout("shiftzoom._fadeIn('"+id+"',"
+o+")",30);}else {if(img.buttons)
{shiftzoom.G(img.ctrlid).style.visibility="visible";
}
if(img.overview&&(img.parentNode.width>img.minwidth|
|img.parentNode.height>img.minheight))
{shiftzoom.G(img.overid).style.visibility="visible";
} if(img.showcoords)
{shiftzoom.G(img.xycoid).style.visibility="visible";
}}        return false; },
    _whilePan : function(e) {
        var img=shiftzoom._shiftzoom;
e=e?e:window.event;
        var
x=Math.max(0,Math.min(img.maxleft,Math.abs(parseInt(
img.parentNode.style.left))-(e.clientX-
img.mouseX)));
        var
y=Math.max(0,Math.min(img.maxtop,Math.abs(parseInt(i
mg.parentNode.style.top))-(e.clientY-img.mouseY)));
        img.parentNode.style.left=(x*-1)+'px';
img.parentNode.style.top=(y*-1)+'px';
img.parentNode.left=(x*-1); img.parentNode.top=(y*-
1); img.mouseX=e.clientX; img.mouseY=e.clientY;
        return false; },
    _stopPan : function() {
        var view, butt, img=shiftzoom._shiftzoom;
document.onmousemove=null; document.onmouseup=null;
        if(img.gecko||img.presto)
{img.style.cursor="move";} else
{img.style.cursor=img.pointer;}if(img.overview) {
view=shiftzoom.G(img.viewid).style;
    view.left=Math.round((Math.abs(parseInt(img.par
entNode.style.left))/(img.parentNode.width/img.minwi
dth))*img.ovsfact)-(img.bmode?2:0)+'px';
```

```
     view.top=Math.round((Math.abs(parseInt(img.pare
ntNode.style.top))/(img.parentNode.height/img.minhei
ght))*img.ovsfact)-(img.bmode?2:0)+'px';
     } shiftzoom._shiftzoom=null; return false;     },
    _startMove : function(e) {      if(!e)
{e=window.event; var view=e.srcElement;}else {var
view=e.target;}     var l=parseInt(view.style.left),
t=parseInt(view.style.top);
cvi_szimage=view.id.substring(0,view.id.indexOf("_")
);      view.style.cursor="default";
view.mouseX=e.clientX; view.mouseY=e.clientY;
        document.onmousemove=shiftzoom._whileMove;
document.onmouseup=shiftzoom._stopMove;
        return false; },
    _whileMove : function(e) {
        if(!e) {e=window.event; var
view=e.srcElement;}else {var view=e.target;}
        var cen=view.id.split("_"),
img=shiftzoom.G(cvi_szimage);
        if(view && cen[cen.length-1]=='view' &&
view.maxleft && view.maxtop) {
            var
l=Math.max(0,Math.min(view.maxleft,Math.abs(parseInt
(view.style.left))+(e.clientX-view.mouseX)));
            var
t=Math.max(0,Math.min(view.maxtop,Math.abs(parseInt(
view.style.top))+(e.clientY-view.mouseY)));
            view.style.left=(l-
(img.bmode?2:0))+'px'; view.style.top=(t-
(img.bmode?2:0))+'px'; view.mouseX=e.clientX;
view.mouseY=e.clientY;
            var
x=Math.max(0,Math.min(img.maxleft,Math.abs(l*(img.pa
rentNode.width/img.minwidth)*(1/img.ovsfact))));
            var
y=Math.max(0,Math.min(img.maxtop,Math.abs(t*(img.par
entNode.height/img.minheight)*(1/img.ovsfact))));
            img.parentNode.style.left=(x*-1)+'px';
img.parentNode.style.top=(y*-1)+'px';
img.parentNode.left=(x*-1); img.parentNode.top=(y*-
1);
        }else {document.onmousemove=null;
document.onmouseup=null;
img.onmousedown=shiftzoom._catchKey;
cvi_szimage=null;}
        return false;
    },
    _stopMove : function()
{document.onmousemove=null; document.onmouseup=null;
shiftzoom.G(cvi_szimage).onmousedown=shiftzoom._catc
hKey; cvi_szimage=null; return false;}}
```

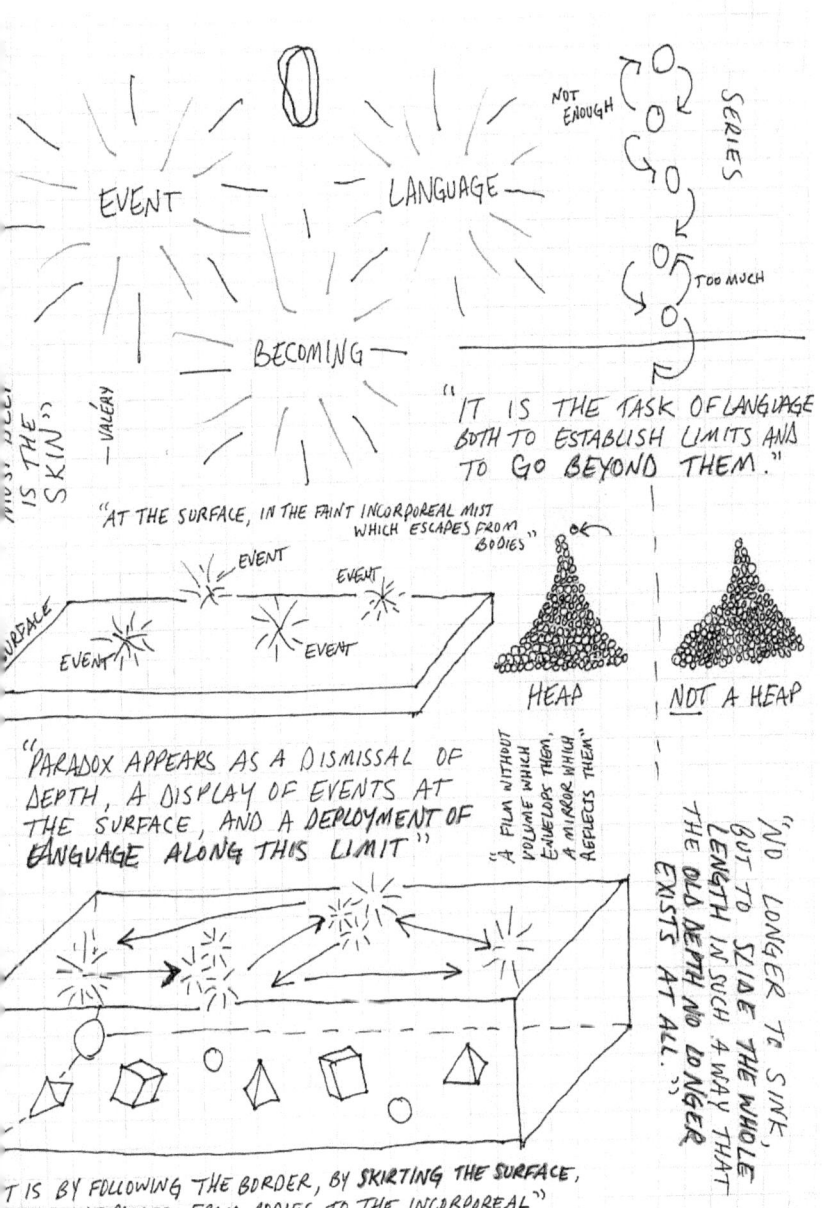

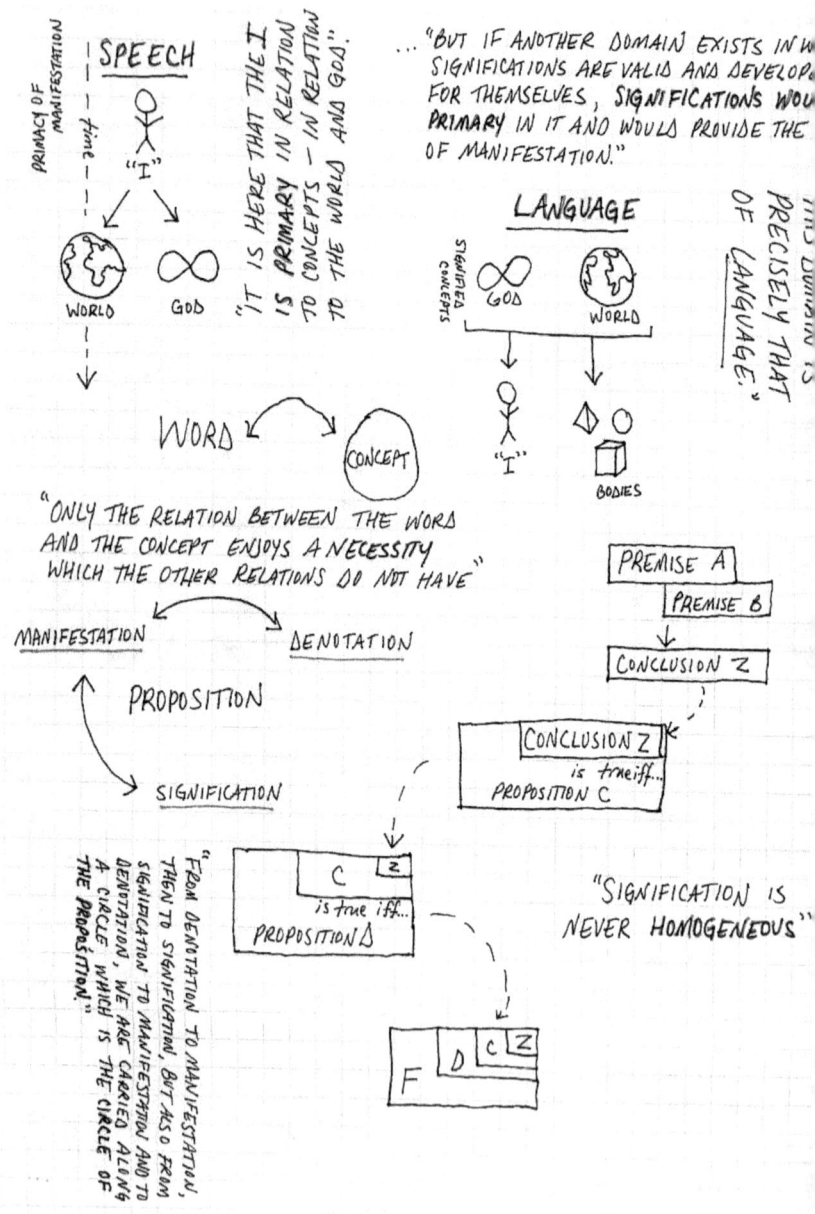

STUTTER

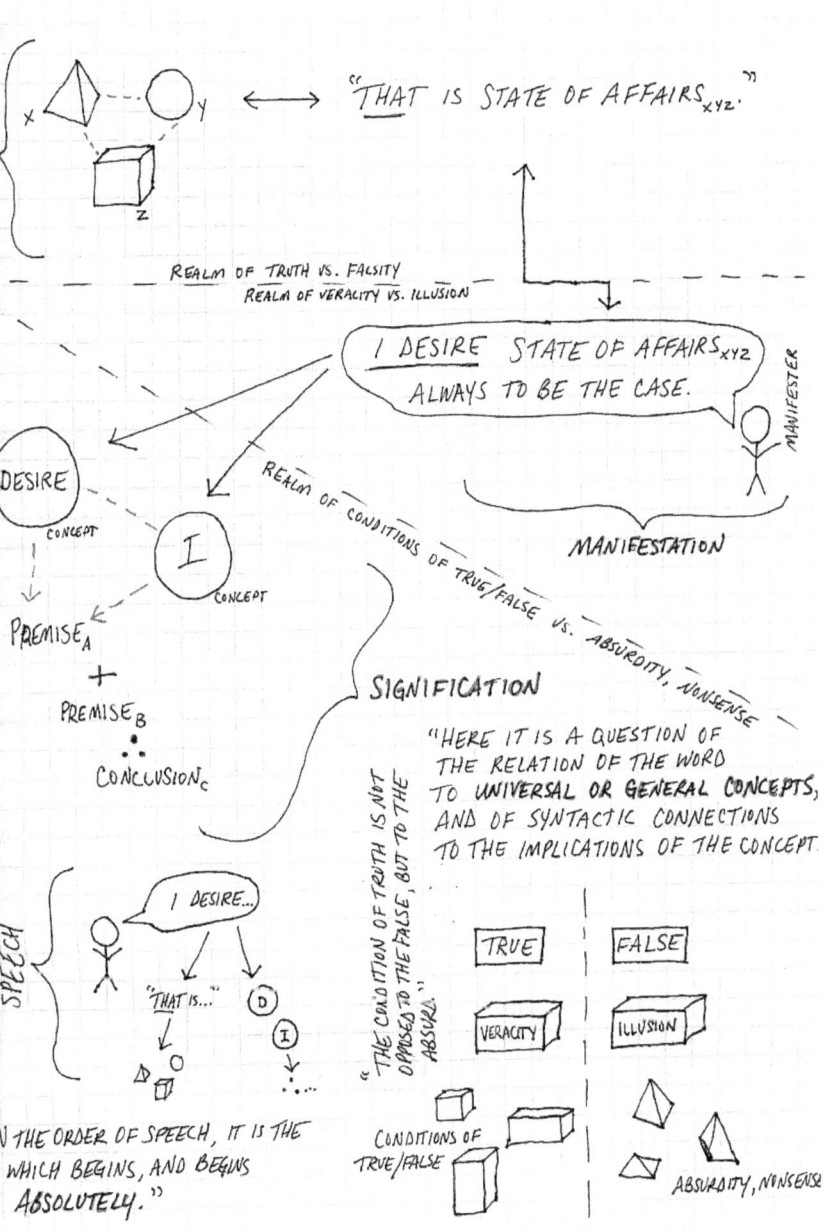

test.html

```html
<html>
<head>
<title>Logic of Sense</title>
<style type="text/css">
/*Default CSS for pan containers*/
.pancontainer{
    position:relative; /*keep this intact*/
    overflow:hidden; /*keep this intact*/
    width:300px;
    height:300px;
    border:0px;
}
body {
    padding:0px;
    margin:0px;
}
#next {
    position:absolute;
    top:100px;
    right:0px;
    z-index:200;
    width:50px;
    height:100px;
    background-color:red;
}
#right-arrow {
    position:absolute;
    top:100px;
    right:0px;
    z-index:100;
    border-bottom:solid 50px transparent;
    border-top:solid 50px transparent;
    border-left:solid 50px black;
}
#previous {
    position:absolute;
    top:100px;
```

```
    left:0px;
    z-index:200;
    width:50px;
    height:100px;
    background-color:red;
}
#left-arrow   {
    position:absolute;
    top:100px;
    left:0px;
    z-index:100;
    border-bottom:solid 50px transparent;
    border-top:solid 50px transparent;
    border-right:solid 50px black;
}
</style>
<script type="text/javascript"
src="http://ajax.googleapis.com/ajax/libs
/jquery/1.4.2/jquery.min.js"></script>
<script type="text/javascript">
function hoverNext(){
    $("#next").css("border-left","solid
50px red");
}
function hoverPrevious(){
    $("#previous").css("border-
right","solid 50px red");
}
function next(){
    $('#previous').replaceWith('<p>i
changed it!</p>');
}
</script>
</head>
<body>
<div id="previous"></div>
<div id="next" onclick="next();"></div>
</body>
</html>
```

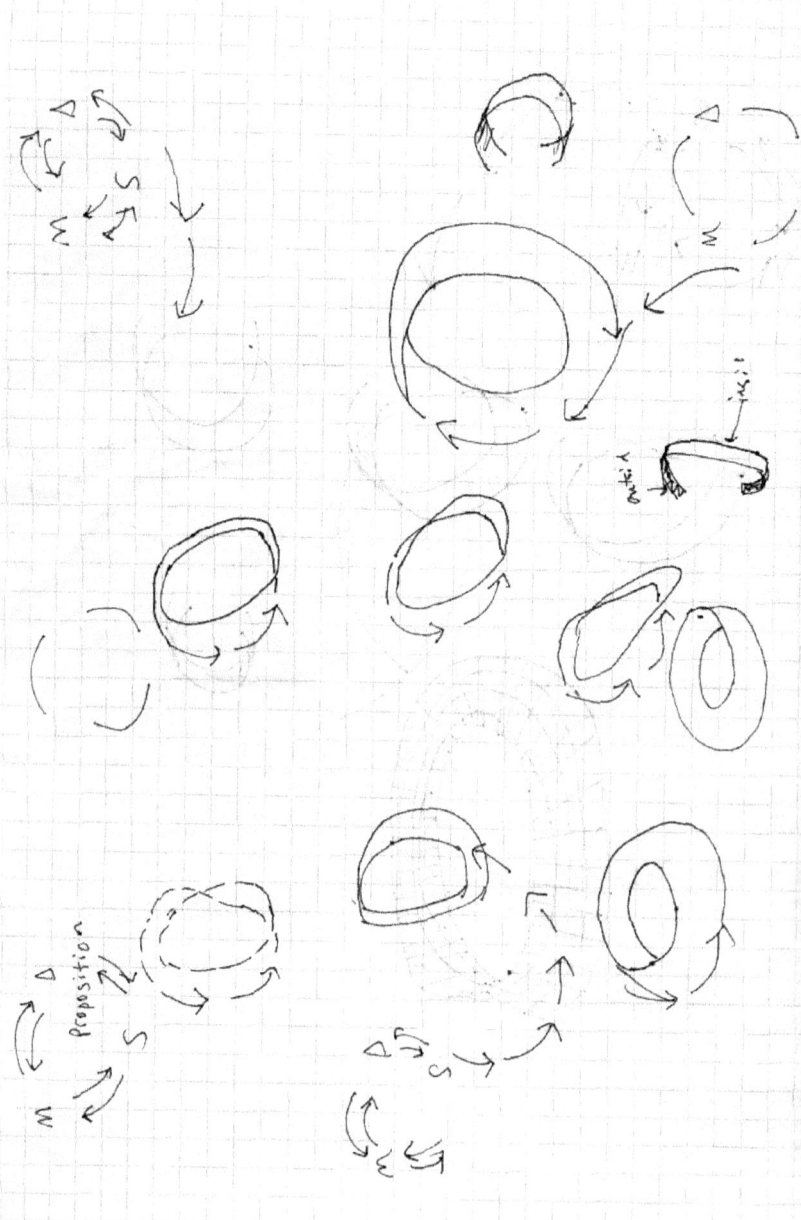

STUTTER

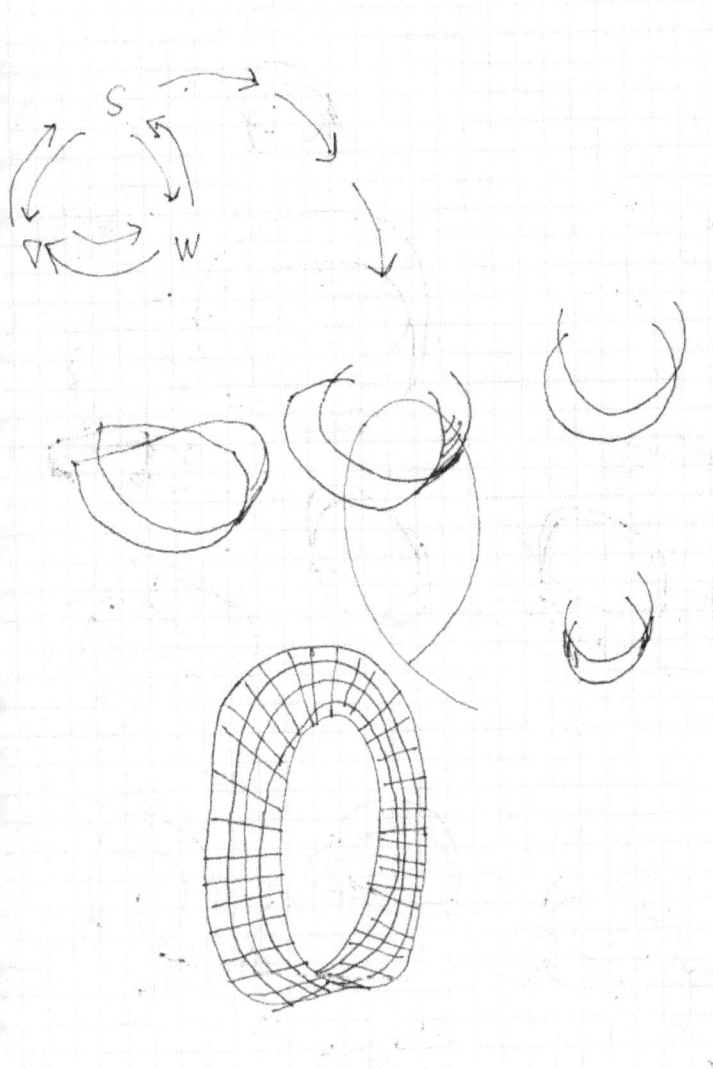

"WHETHER WE OUGHT TO BE CONTENT WITH THESE THREE DIMENSIONS OF T[HE] PROPOSITION, OR WHETHER WE SHOULD ADD A FOURTH — WHICH WOULD BE SEN[SE]"

DENOTATION

WORD → THING

Where is sense located?

"ALL DENOTATION PRESUPPOSES SENSE... WE POSITION OURSELVES STRAIGHT AWAY WITHIN SENSE WHENEVER WE DENOTE"

"I DESIRE..."

"SENSE RESIDES [IN] THE BELIEFS (OR...) OF THE PERSON W[HO] EXPRESSES HERSE[LF]"

MANIFESTATION

SIGNIFICATION

FORMS → POSSIBILITY

"AN INCORPOREAL, COMPLEX, AND IRREDUCIBLE ENTITY, AT THE SURFACE OF THINGS, A **PURE EVENT** WHICH INHERES OR SUBSISTS IN THE PROPOSITION"

CONCEPT / WORD
BODY

"BY WHATEVER MANNER ONE DEFINES FORM, IT IS AN OD[D] PROCEDURE SINCE IT INVOLVE[S] RISING FROM THE CONDITIONE[D] TO THE CONDITION, IN ORDER T[O] THINK OF THE CONDITION AS TH[E] SIMPLE POSSIBILITY OF THE CONDITIONED"

"SENSE IS THE FOURTH DIMENSION OF THE PROPOSITION."

MANIFESTATION → DENOTAT[ION] → SIGNIFICATION

demo-ajax.html

```html
<html>
    <head>
        <title>Image Annotations</title>
        <style type="text/css"
media="all">@import
"css/annotation.css";</style>
        <script type="text/javascript"
src="js/jquery-1.3.2.js"></script>
        <script type="text/javascript"
src="js/jquery-ui-1.7.1.js"></script>
        <script type="text/javascript"
src="js/jquery.annotate.js"></script>

        <script language="javascript">
            $(window).load(function() {

    $("#toAnnotate").annotateImage({
                    getUrl: "get.html",
                    saveUrl: "save.html",
                    deleteUrl:
"delete.html",
                    editable: true
                });
            });
        </script>
    </head>
    <body>
        <div>
            <img id="toAnnotate"
src="images/trafalgar-square-
annotated.jpg" alt="Trafalgar Square"
width="600" height="398" />
        </div>
    </body>
</html>
```

imagepanner.js

```
/* Simple Image Panner and Zoomer (March 11th, 10)
* This notice must stay intact for usage
* Author: Dynamic Drive at
http://www.dynamicdrive.com/
* Visit http://www.dynamicdrive.com/ for full source
code
*/

// v1.1 (March 25th, 10): Updated with ability to
zoom in/out of image

jQuery.noConflict()

var ddimagepanner={

    magnifyicons: ['magnify.gif','magnify2.gif',
24,23], //set path to zoom in/out images, plus their
dimensions
    maxzoom: 4, //set maximum zoom level (from 1x)

    init:function($, $img, options){
        var s=options
        s.imagesize=[$img.width(), $img.height()]
        s.oimagesize=[$img.width(), $img.height()]
//always remember image's original size
        s.pos=(s.pos=="center")? [-
(s.imagesize[0]/2-s.wrappersize[0]/2), -
(s.imagesize[1]/2-s.wrappersize[1]/2)] : [0, 0]
//initial coords of image
        s.pos=[Math.floor(s.pos[0]),
Math.floor(s.pos[1])]
        $img.css({position:'absolute',
left:s.pos[0], top:s.pos[1]})
        if (s.canzoom=="yes"){ //enable image
zooming?
            s.dragcheck={h:
(s.wrappersize[0]>s.imagesize[0])? false:true,
v:(s.wrappersize[1]>s.imagesize[1])? false:true}
//check if image should be draggable horizon and
vertically
            s.$statusdiv=$('<div
style="position:absolute;color:white;background:#353
535;padding:2px 10px;font-
size:12px;visibility:hidden">1x
Magnify</div>').appendTo(s.$pancontainer) //create
DIV to show current magnify level
            s.$statusdiv.css({left:0,
top:s.wrappersize[1]-s.$statusdiv.outerHeight(),
```

```
              display:'none', visibility:'visible'})
            this.zoomfunct($, $img, s)
        }
        this.dragimage($, $img, s)
    },

    dragimage:function($, $img, s){
        $img.mousedown(function(e){
            s.pos=[parseInt($img.css('left')),
parseInt($img.css('top'))]
            var xypos=[e.clientX, e.clientY]
            $img.bind('mousemove.dragstart',
function(e){
                var pos=s.pos,
imagesize=s.imagesize, wrappersize=s.wrappersize
                var dx=e.clientX-xypos[0]
//distance to move horizontally
                var dy=e.clientY-xypos[1]
//vertically
                s.dragcheck={h:
(wrappersize[0]>imagesize[0])? false:true,
v:(wrappersize[1]>imagesize[1])? false:true}
                if (s.dragcheck.h==true) //allow
dragging horizontally?
                    var newx=(dx>0)? Math.min(0,
pos[0]+dx) : Math.max(-imagesize[0]+wrappersize[0],
pos[0]+dx) //Set horizonal bonds. dx>0 indicates
drag right versus left
                if (s.dragcheck.v==true) //allow
dragging vertically?
                    var newy=(dy>0)? Math.min(0,
s.pos[1]+dy) : Math.max(-
imagesize[1]+wrappersize[1], pos[1]+dy) //Set
vertical bonds. dy>0 indicates drag downwards versus
up
                $img.css({left:(typeof
newx!="undefined")? newx : pos[0], top:(typeof
newy!="undefined")? newy : pos[1]})
                return false //cancel default drag
action
            })
            return false //cancel default drag
action
        })
        $(document).bind('mouseup', function(e){
            $img.unbind('mousemove.dragstart')
        })
    },

    zoomfunct:function($, $img, s){
        var magnifyicons=this.magnifyicons
```

```
            var $zoomimages=$('<img
src="'+magnifyicons[0]+'" /><img
src="'+magnifyicons[1]+'" />')
                .css({width:magnifyicons[2],
height:magnifyicons[3], cursor:'pointer',
zIndex:1000, position:'absolute',
                            top:s.wrappersize[1]-
magnifyicons[3]-1, left:s.wrappersize[0]-
magnifyicons[2]-3, opacity:0.7
                })
                .attr("title", "Zoom Out")
                .appendTo(s.$pancontainer)

    $zoomimages.eq(0).css({left:parseInt($zoomimage
s.eq(0).css('left'))-magnifyicons[2]-3, opacity:1})
//position "zoom in" image
                .attr("title", "Zoom In")
        $zoomimages.click(function(e){ //assign
click behavior to zoom images
                var $zimg=$(this) //reference image
clicked on
                var curzoom=s.curzoom //get current
zoom level
                var
zoomtype=($zimg.attr("title").indexOf("In")!=-1)?
"in" : "out"
                if (zoomtype=="in" &&
s.curzoom==ddimagepanner.maxzoom || zoomtype=="out"
&& s.curzoom==1) //exit if user at either ends of
magnify levels
                    return
                var basepos=[s.pos[0]/curzoom,
s.pos[1]/curzoom]
                var newzoom=(zoomtype=="out")?
Math.max(1, curzoom-1) :
Math.min(ddimagepanner.maxzoom, curzoom+1) //get new
zoom level
                $zoomimages.css("opacity", 1)
                if (newzoom==1) //if zoom level is 1x,
dim "zoom out" image
                    $zoomimages.eq(1).css("opacity",
0.7)
                else if
(newzoom==ddimagepanner.maxzoom) //if zoom level is
max level, dim "zoom in" image
                    $zoomimages.eq(0).css("opacity",
0.7)
                clearTimeout(s.statustimer)
                s.$statusdiv.html(newzoom+"x
Magnify").show() //show current zoom status/level
                var nd=[s.oimagesize[0]*newzoom,
```

```
            s.oimagesize[1]*newzoom]
              var newpos=[basepos[0]*newzoom,
basepos[1]*newzoom]
              newpos=[(zoomtype=="in" &&
s.wrappersize[0]>s.imagesize[0] || zoomtype=="out"
&& s.wrappersize[0]>nd[0])? s.wrappersize[0]/2-
nd[0]/2 : Math.max(-nd[0]+s.wrappersize[0],
newpos[0]),
              (zoomtype=="in" &&
s.wrappersize[1]>s.imagesize[1] || zoomtype=="out"
&& s.wrappersize[1]>nd[1])? s.wrappersize[1]/2-
nd[1]/2 : Math.max(-nd[1]+s.wrappersize[1],
newpos[1])]
              $img.animate({width:nd[0],
height:nd[1], left:newpos[0], top:newpos[1]},
function(){

    s.statustimer=setTimeout(function(){s.$statusdi
v.hide()}, 500)
              })
              s.imagesize=nd
              s.curzoom=newzoom
              s.pos=[newpos[0], newpos[1]]
          })
      }

}


jQuery.fn.imgmover=function(options){
    var $=jQuery
    return this.each(function(){ //return jQuery
obj
        if (this.tagName!="IMG")
             return true //skip to next matched
element
        var $imgref=$(this)
        if (parseInt(this.style.width)>0 &&
parseInt(this.style.height)>0) //if image has
explicit CSS width/height defined
             ddimagepanner.init($, $imgref,
options)
        else if (this.complete){ //account for IE
not firing image.onload
             ddimagepanner.init($, $imgref,
options)
         }
         else{
             $imgref.bind('load', function(){
                 ddimagepanner.init($, $imgref,
options)
```

```
            })
        }
    })
}


jQuery(document).ready(function($){ //By default
look for DIVs with class="pancontainer"
    var $pancontainer=$('div.pancontainer')
    $pancontainer.each(function(){
        var $this=$(this).css({position:'relative',
overflow:'hidden', cursor:'move'})
        var $img=$this.find('img:eq(0)') //image to
pan
        var options={$pancontainer:$this,
pos:$this.attr('data-orient'), curzoom:1,
canzoom:$this.attr('data-canzoom'),
wrappersize:[$this.width(), $this.height()]}
        $img.imgmover(options)
    })
})
```

index.html

```
<html>
<head>
<title>Logic of Sense</title>
<style type="text/css">
/*Default CSS for pan containers*/
.pancontainer{
    position:relative; /*keep this intact*/
    overflow:hidden; /*keep this intact*/
    width:300px;
    height:300px;
    border:0px;
}
body {
    padding:0px;
    margin:0px;
}
#next {
    position:absolute;
    top:100px;
    right:0px;
    z-index:200;
    width:50px;
    height:100px;
    background-color:red;
}
#right-arrow {
    position:absolute;
```

```css
    top:100px;
    right:0px;
    z-index:100;
    border-bottom:solid 50px transparent;
    border-top:solid 50px transparent;
    border-left:solid 50px black;
}
#previous {
    position:absolute;
    top:100px;
    left:0px;
    z-index:200;
    width:50px;
    height:100px;
    background-color:red;
}
#left-arrow  {
    position:absolute;
    top:100px;
    left:0px;
    z-index:100;
    border-bottom:solid 50px transparent;
    border-top:solid 50px transparent;
    border-right:solid 50px black;
}
</style>
```
```html
<script type="text/javascript"
src="http://ajax.googleapis.com/ajax/libs/jquery/1.4.2/jquery.min.js"></script>
<script type="text/javascript" src="imagepanner.js">
/***************************************************
* Simple Image Panner and Zoomer- (c) Dynamic Drive
DHTML code library (www.dynamicdrive.com)
* This notice MUST stay intact for legal use
* Visit Dynamic Drive at
http://www.dynamicdrive.com/ for this script and
100s more
***************************************************/
</script>
<script type="text/javascript">
function hoverNext(){
    $("#next").css("border-left","solid 50px red");
}
function hoverPrevious(){
    $("#previous").css("border-right","solid 50px red");
}
function next(){
    $('#previous').replaceWith('<p>i changed it!</p>');
}
```

```html
</script>
</head>
<body>
<div id="previous"></div>
<span onclick="next();"><div id="next"></div></span>
<div class="pancontainer" data-orient="center" data-canzoom="yes" style="width:100%; height:100%;">
    <img class="sketch" src="los001_small.png" style="width:609px; height:754px" />
</div>
</body>
</html>
```

index1.html

```html
<html>
<head>
<style type="text/css">
/*Default CSS for pan containers*/
.pancontainer{
    position:relative; /*keep this intact*/
    border:0px;
    overflow:hidden; /*keep this intact*/
}
body {
    padding:0px;
    margin:0px;
}
#next {
    position:absolute;
    top:100px;
    right:0px;
    z-index:100;
    border-bottom:solid 50px transparent;
    border-top:solid 50px transparent;
    border-left:solid 50px black;
}
#previous  {
    position:absolute;
    top:100px;
    left:0px;
    z-index:100;
    border-bottom:solid 50px transparent;
    border-top:solid 50px transparent;
    border-right:solid 50px black;
}
</style>
<script type="text/javascript" src="http://ajax.googleapis.com/ajax/libs/jquery/1.4.2/jquery.min.js"></script>
```

```html
<script type="text/javascript"
src="shiftzoom.js"></script>
</head>
<body>
<div id="previous"
onmouseover="hoverPrevious();"></div>
<div id="next" onmouseover="hoverNext();"
onclick="next();"></div>
<div><img
onLoad="shiftzoom.add(this,{showcoords:true,zoom:100
});" src="los001_small.png" style="width:609px;
height:754px" />
</div>
</body>
</html>
```

save.html

W. dreams, like Phaedrus, of an army of thinker-friends, thinker-lovers. He dreams of a thought-army, a thought-pack, which would storm the philosophical Houses of Parliament. He dreams of Tartars from the philosophical steppes, of thought-barbarians, thought-outsiders. What distances would shine in their eyes!

~Lars Iyer

www.babelworkinggroup.org

www.ingramcontent.com/pod-product-compliance
Lightning Source LLC
Chambersburg PA
CBHW070849160426
43192CB00012B/2370